Taming the Internet

Your Guide To Getting The Most Out Of The Internet In New Orleans

by

Charlyn Keating

Cover design and illustrations by

Kathryn Andries Muse

Prytania Press

To Patricia, See you online! Charlyn Keating

Taming the Internet: Your Guide To Getting The Most Out Of The Internet in New Orleans

Published by:
Prytania Press
P.O. Box 52173
New Orleans, LA 70152
prytaniapress@email.com

Visit our Web site:
http://www.learntheweb.com

ISBN 1-893328-25-2
Printed in the United States of America
First Printing, November, 1998
10 9 8 7 6 5 4 3 2 1

Here's what others are saying about Charlyn Keating's *Taming The Internet*:

*"**Taming the Internet** is a must for every person who treads in fear of the electronic age. The Internet comes to life in simple terms that transform a scary maze of technology into a friendly tool that can be mastered by all.*

Joseph A. Grace, Jr.
President, New Orleans Technology Council

"Charlyn Keating has helped our viewers navigate the Web for the past two years. Now her readers can get a private lesson from Channel 4's computer expert to help them make sense of communicating in the 21st century."

Eric Paulsen, WWL-TV

*"**Taming the Internet** is like having someone literally guide you step by step through all the technology jargon that at times can be intimidating. It puts you at ease when you access the Internet and then after a few sessions you will feel like you're an expert. This book is so user-friendly and so informative that anyone can benefit from its use."*

Mark Lewis, founder, Communique

About the Author

Charlyn Keating has spent the past 10 years as a professional in the computer industry. Her roles have included multimedia producer, software programmer, project manager, computer instructor, and technology consultant. Currently, she is Internet Marketing Manager at Examco, the world's leader in technology-based training. Her team is responsible for the design and development of the Examco corporate Web site (www.examco.com), and Examco's pioneering Web-based training program. She first logged on to the Internet 7 years ago, and continues to watch it evolve.

Ms. Keating received a Communications degree from the University of Texas. As Executive Director of Futurekids Computer Learning Center in Metairie in the first half of the 90s, she was interviewed several times on television as an industry expert, on topics such as the Year 2000 Problem, Internet fraud, and computer education. Currently she appears weekly on WWL-TV's Eyewitness Morning News as the technology correspondent. She wrote this book for her parents, who both wish she had more time to show them around the Internet.

To Mom and Dad,
who provide
constant encouragement,
fierce loyalty,
and unconditional love

Acknowledgements

I owe a debt of gratitude to many people including:

Arthur Hardy, for being one of the first to believe in the project;

Mom, for all those delicious home-cooked meals;

Dad, for his editing help, and for reminding me that he can't download files;

my grandmother Juanita McCune, for her willingness to help out every time;

Biker Bob, for buying the first copy;

Kathryn Andries Muse, for her charming illustrations and undying patience;

Susan Pickle and Shawn LaVergne, for their editing and layout expertise;

Mark Lewis, who can change a flat tire **and** give technical advice;

Verio Gulf South, my wonderfully reliable ISP;

Joe Grace, for stepping in at the eleventh hour with tremendous inspiration;

and Eric Paulsen, Sally-Ann Roberts, Dionne Butler, and the crew at WWL, for making me feel quite at home. Thank you all!

Contents

Part I: The Basics

Section II: Getting the Hang of It

Section III: Staying Safe

Section IV: Take a Guided Tour of the Web

Introduction

Welcome to ***Taming The Internet***. If you are new to the Internet and a little confused about where to start, you are in the right place. This book contains all the basic knowledge you need.

The Internet is an exciting place to be. Connecting the Internet has been described as "opening a window to the world." Once you are online, you have access to a whole new universe of information, news, advice, entertainment, and friends.

Exploring the Internet for the first time can be overwhelming. There is so much to see and do, you won't know where to start. The entire Internet is "under construction" constantly. A site you visit today will be gone tomorrow, and five new sites will appear. You will hear people speak a whole new language. Some people won't be very friendly or patient. Con men have set up shop alongside legitimate businesses. Everything is new, confusing, and a little bit intimidating.

I wrote this book so I could give you a personal tour of the Internet. This book is different from other books for two important reasons. First, all of the other books I've seen load you down with far more information than you really need.

How much information is too much? Well, navigating the Internet is similar to driving a car. You don't have to become a master mechanic. You learn how to turn the key, how the pedals work, and what the rules of the road are. You don't have to learn how the engine works. Use this book to get comfortable with Internet basics first, and learn the rest later.

Second, this book is written specifically for everyone in the metro New Orleans area. Unlike national Internet books, I don't have to be vague and tell you to "go look it up." I can give very specific, local information, including local Web sites.

This book is written in English. I don't assume you know anything about the Internet. All of the "techie terms" I use are explained in the glossary.

My best advice to you is this: give yourself plenty of time to learn. Remember that the Internet was built 30 years ago by, well, nerds. It is still being "reinvented" every single day. Even people who have been on the Internet for many years get confused by all of the new developments.

Give yourself time to learn and explore. Be patient with yourself. Don't expect to understand everything right away. Ask for help. There are many people on the Internet willing to lend a hand. It will get easier.

Once you are on the 'net, stop by our Web site:

`http://www.learntheweb.com`

You will find updates to the book, new Web sites to try, and a whole community of people learning their way around the Internet. Stick around long enough, and soon you will be giving other people advice on how to navigate the World Wide Web!

How To Use This Book

This book is not a school textbook. You don't have to read the entire book from beginning to end, and there won't be a test.

I suggest reading the first three sections entirely. They contain some basic, important information.

Part IV is a directory of interesting sites in many categories, including local sites. They will point you to some of the most useful, informative sites on the Web.

Part V is a glossary of online terms. You can refer to this anytime you see a word, either in this book, online, or in a magazine, that you don't fully understand.

The Appendices include some reference information for later.

Here are some standards used throughout this book:

- Web site addresses look like this: `www.example.com`. Type them into your browser exactly as they appear in the book. In case you don't feel like typing all those addresses, we've done it for you at our Web site. Just go to `www.learntheweb.com`.

- Menu commands in your computer software (that you would click on using your mouse) are shown like this: **File⇨Options**.
- Keyboard keys that you would press are shown like this: **RETURN**.
- Special sections appear through the book:

Expert Advice

You can avoid a pitfall by reading these.

On The Web

You can find more information on a topic at the Web sites listed.

Impress Your Friends!

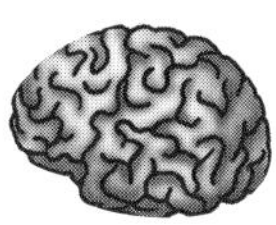

These sections contain interesting facts you don't need to know. They are useful for impressing friends and family members!

Please note: The step-by-step instructions are provided for Netscape Navigator version 4.0 for the Mac and Microsoft Internet Explorer version 4.0 for the PC. The screen shots are from the PC version of Internet Explorer. Instructions are provided for these browsers, since the majority of the people reading this book will be using one of the two. This does not necessarily reflect my personal preferences. If you have a different browser, or a different version of these two browsers, your experience will vary slightly from the instructions given in the book.

Feedback

I really want to hear from you. Visit the Web site at www.learntheweb.com to register your comments, complaints, favorite Web sites, and questions. Unfortunately, I am not able to answer everybody's individual questions. However, I will answer questions on the site, so ask away! Chances are many other people will want to see the answer to your question, but they were just too shy to ask!

All of the Web sites included in this book were valid as of publication. However, the Internet changes every day. Please let me know if you find a site that doesn't work anymore. I will post alternatives at www.learntheweb.com.

Ten Reasons Why You Should Be Online

1. Keep in touch with friends, relatives, and business associates (even if they are thousands of miles away).

2. Experience the world's greatest art, literature, and music.

3. Show your kids that learning online is a lot more fun than watching TV.

4. ***Meet new friends you can talk to twenty-four hours a day, about anything from tattoos to mutual funds.***

5. Shop in a boutique in Italy and a bazaar in Turkey in the same afternoon.

6. 

Receive personalized news, sports, and weather delivered to your desktop daily (even hourly).

7. CLIP COUPONS, ENTER CONTESTS, GET FREE SAMPLES, AND DOWNLOAD FREE SOFTWARE.

8. 

Explore historic documents, speeches, and photographs.

9. Play games with dozens of other people, in real time, day or night.

10. 

FIND THE LOWEST RATES ON AIRFARE, HOTELS, CRUISE SHIPS, AND VACATION PACKAGES.

PART I: The Basics

In this section, you will discover how to:

- connect your computer to the Internet
- get the software you need
- access the Internet, even if you don't own a computer
- surf the World Wide Web

How Do I Get Online?

If you don't already have access to the Internet through your company or school, the first thing you will need to do is to get connected. You will need three things: the right hardware, the right software, and an account with an ISP, an Internet Service Provider. Let's go over each of these.

1) Hardware

Hardware refers to all of the equipment you can see and touch. Typically, you will need a **computer** and a **modem**.

Computer

Prices for computer systems have dropped radically over the past year. You can get a brand new system, with all of the power, bells, and whistles you need, plus everything you need to surf the Web, for under $1000. The details about what you get for that price change more quickly than the weather, so we won't go into detail about megabytes and gigabytes here. Choose a computer that has been released in the last six months to a year, and you will be fine.

If this is your first computer purchase, choose a name brand. Ask your friends and neighbors for recommendations. Many people choose Compaq, Dell, or Gateway 2000, and there are other good brands as well. Find out what warranty and service agreements are available. Many computer retailers offer free on-site service, which means they will send a repairman to your home if anything goes wrong. (If something does go wrong, you won't want to ship the computer out of state to have it fixed!) Ask before you buy.

Do I Really Need A Computer?

If you are not ready to invest in a computer, there are other, even less expensive ways to access the Internet.

WebTV

For about $250, you can buy a small black box, which can be attached to a regular TV set. WebTV lets you surf the Web from your sofa with the remote control. For about $70 more, you can add a wireless keyboard for sending e-mail. WebTV also comes with built-in parental guidance software.

WebTV is convenient and inexpensive, but it is not a computer. You won't be able to download software or run other programs. Also, it has been slower to support the more advanced features some Web sites use. So you may have trouble viewing some sites.

WebTV may soon have some competition. America Online recently purchased NetChannel and will be offering a box and service similar to WebTV. Keep an eye on your mailbox for details.

CyberCafe

If you just want to get your feet wet before you purchase anything, try a CyberCafe. They have been popping up all over the New Orleans area. Usually you can get Internet access free, or for a dollar or so an hour.

Library

The New Orleans Public Library offers Internet access, free, to anyone who has a library card. You can use one of the free e-mail services for your own e-mail address (see *"Free E-mail Accounts"*). You can even download software (floppy disks are available for $1.00, or you can bring your own). Printing is 15 cents per page.

The St. Tammany and Jefferson Parish Library systems offer similar services. Public Internet access at libraries is a wonderful public service, allowing access to everyone in the community.

Modem

With a computer, you will need a modem. A modem is the device that allows your computer to communicate with other computers, using a standard telephone line. If you have purchased a computer in the last couple of years, chances are it came with a modem already installed.

> **IMPRESS YOUR FRIENDS!**
>
> **Modems are like translators between computers and the telephone system. Computers understand digital information (numbers), and telephones understand analog information (waves). A modem takes signals from a computer and "modulates" them (turns them into waves, which sound to us like screeching). The modem on the other end of the line "demodulates" them (turns them back into numbers). That's where the word "modem" comes from: modulate and demodulate.**

Modems are rated by their speed. The larger the number, the faster the modem can send and receive "bits" of information. I recommend at least a 28.8 Kbps modem to access the Web, although they come in speeds as high as 56 Kbps. A faster modem is nearly always worth the price. If you are surfing the Web or downloading files, a faster modem will dramatically decrease the amount of time it takes, therefore giving you a more enjoyable online experience.

Take some time to read the documentation that comes with your modem. Modems can be tricky to set up and get working properly. If you need help, ask your computer dealer or a knowledgeable friend.

EXPERT ADVICE

If you have call waiting, turn it off before you connect to the Internet with the modem, or an incoming call will disconnect you from the Web. Type *70 then a comma in front of the phone number your modem dials, like this: `*70, 555-5555`**. This will disable call waiting for that one call. As soon as you hang up, call waiting will work again.**

(If you are connecting from an office with multiple users, you might want a faster, more direct connection to the Internet. Talk to your ISP about your options.)

The modem connects to an ordinary phone line. Just remember, while you are on the modem, no one else can use the same phone line to send or receive calls. Callers will receive a busy signal or get sent to voice mail. (This can be a problem especially if you need help with your connection, and you don't have a second phone line to call tech support.) For this reason, you may want to consider getting a second phone line for the computer.

2) Internet Access

Next, you will need to subscribe to a service that will give you access to the Internet. Generally, you will use your modem and a phone line from home to dial in to their computers. You have two basic choices: you can choose a large, commercial online service like AOL, or a local or regional Internet Service Provider (an ISP).

Commercial Online Service

Large commercial online services, like America Online, CompuServe, and the Microsoft Network, offer a more organized environment than you will often find on the Web. These services offer their own private network of information, like technical support forums, interest groups, and magazine articles. They will also provide you with a gateway to the Internet.

Commercial online services are often referred to as "the Internet with training wheels." As you spend more time online, you may find that you are outgrowing the service.

The Good News:	The Bad News:
· More organized environment · Some services can be easier to use · Startup disks are everywhere and make signing up very easy · Hundreds of members-only forums, software libraries, and chat rooms · Technical support is available online or through the telephone · Areas devoted to kids	· You may have trouble seeing some sites · You may have trouble connecting at peak times and connecting at higher modem speeds · They may censor your e-mail · They may limit the parts of the Internet you have access to · You may see full-page ads · You may receive a lot of junk e-mail

ISP

At one time, the large commercial online services were the only way most people could access online information. People signed up because of the members-only network of information they offered. Now, the same information (and more) can be found on the Web. Many local and regional Internet Service Providers (ISPs) can give you direct access to the Internet.

If you choose to sign up with an ISP, you will have direct access to all that the Internet offers. There are no training wheels, so it might be a bit confusing at first. They do not provide you with content, so you will have to find it on the Web. But once you get the hang of it, you will be able to experience everything on the Web. Nothing will hold you back!

There are two categories of ISPs: larger, regional (or national) providers; and smaller, local ISPs.

Choose a smaller, local ISP if you are looking for more personalized service. Or perhaps you have a small business and need help creating your own Web site; a local ISP can help.

Choose a larger, regional or national provider if you travel and need to access your e-mail or the Web from the road. A national provider will be more likely to give you a local number to dial from wherever you are in the country, saving you long-distance charges. (Some local ISPs will offer you an 800 number to use; ask your ISP to be sure).

Choosing An Access Provider

ISPs are not created equal. Some provide better service than others, and some are more reliable than others. They may offer different services. They may be more helpful with technical support or customer support. It is important to choose a provider that is right for you. Don't just choose the cheapest one. A good ISP is worth an extra $5 per month.

Check *Appendix C* for a list of ISPs. You may want to ask your friends and business associates how happy they are with their service. Call and ask questions before you sign up:

How much are the monthly fees?

Monthly fees should generally be a flat rate of about $20 per month for unlimited access time, any time of the day. You don't want to pay by the hour. Find out if there are any additional charges, such as a **setup charge**, or extra connection fees for faster modems. You should be able to find an ISP that will provide you with free setup and free software.

What kind of software will I need?

Most ISPs will provide you with a startup disk, including all the software you need. Ask the ISP what software they will provide, and what you will have to find yourself. Ask if they will provide written instructions to help you get started.

Find out if they require you to use a particular browser or e-mail program. Some ISPs require you to use their software, instead of the most popular software, which means you might be missing out on some features.

Will I have a local phone number to call?

You will need a **local phone number** to access the Internet. If you travel, ask if they have local numbers in other areas of the country (or at least a toll-free number you can use when you're on the road). Find out if any extra charges apply when you are using their toll-free number.

Will I be able to get through during busy times?

Some companies have more customers then they can handle, which means you might have trouble getting through to the ISP, especially during peak times. Ask how many subscribers they have for each incoming phone line. If it is more than 10 to 1, you may have trouble getting connected in the evenings.

Try to get a free trial period, and call in at different times of the day to see if you can get through. If you cannot try the service free, make sure you can cancel if you are not satisfied.

Is free technical support provided?

Toll-free, 24-hour a day technical support (manned by live human beings) is ideal. If you are having problems in the middle of the night, you will want to be able to reach a real person. At the very least, make sure you have a local or toll-free phone number to call for help. Call it a few times to make sure you can get through, and are not put on hold for too long.

What modem speed do they support?

Make sure the ISP will allow you to connect at your modem's highest speed. There should not be any extra charges for connecting at a high speed. Make sure they support your modem, whether it is 14.4, 28.8, 33.6, or faster. The latest modems are

56 Kbps, and there are two incompatible types: x2 and K56Flex. Find out what kind of modem and speed you have, and ask the ISP if it is supported.

If you are setting up a connection for a business, make sure they have the capability to provide faster access, like ADSL, T1, or T3.

What services do they provide?

Make sure they offer all the services you are likely to need. Besides e-mail and access to the Web, there are other applications like FTP, Telnet, Usenet, and IRC. Do they offer these as well? Even if you are not sure if you will use them, it is best to find an ISP that offers all of the services.

Do they offer free home pages?

Even if you are not thinking about it yet, you might want to put up your own page on the Web later. Most ISPs will offer space on their servers for your own home page, at no additional charge. Ask if this is available, and find out how much space you will have. Most ISPs will offer 5-10 megabytes free of charge. Make sure you know what the charges are if you go over that limit, or if you put up a Web site for a business.

Do I have to sign a long-term contract?

Find out what you have to do to cancel the service. Do you have to sign a long-term contract? Do you have to pre-pay for a year in advance? Make sure there are no penalties for canceling your service.

List of Service Providers

Check *Appendix C* for a list of commercial online services and ISPs (national, regional, and local).

3) Software

Software refers to programs that run on your system. They are like a set of instructions that tell the computer what to do. There is a lot of Internet software out there to use, but here are the two basic types of programs to get you started:

Browser

You will need a browser to get around on the World Wide Web. The browser is the software that displays Web pages on your screen.

Get A Browser

Browsers are usually free. If you have purchased a computer recently, you probably already have a browser installed on your hard drive. A shortcut to the browser will appear on your desktop. When you sign up with an ISP for Internet access, they will more than likely give you a browser. You can also **download** the browser you would like to use from the Internet.

Some ISPs have their own **proprietary** browsers. With some effort, you can usually switch to a more popular browser after you are up and running. (If you are using WebTV, you are required to use their browser.)

Which One To Choose?

Choosing a browser is really just a matter of personal preference. Right now the two most popular browsers are Microsoft's Internet Explorer and Netscape's Navigator. In theory, all browsers display Web pages the same way. In practice, this is not always the case. Both Netscape Navigator and Internet Explorer support their own extra features.

Many people build extra features into their sites that are only supported in one browser or another. You will usually see a part of their site that says, "Best viewed with IE or Navigator." But in general, you can still visit and read most sites with either browser; you just might miss some of the bells and whistles. And, most larger companies will design sites so that both browsers are fully supported. You can download a copy of either browser at the Web sites shown below:

Netscape Navigator
www.netscape.com/download

Internet Explorer
www.microsoft.com/ie/download

Besides the two most popular browsers, you have other choices. Some alternative browsers are listed below. You can download them at the addresses shown:

Opera
traviata.nta.no/opera.htm

Cello
www.law.cornell.edu/cello/cellotop.html

NCSA Mosaic
www.ncsa.uiuc.edu/SDG/Software/Mosaic/NCSAMosaicHome

ON THE WEB

For even more alternatives, including browsers for different systems like Amiga and OS/2, check out:

browserwatch.internet.com/browsers.html

E-Mail

Besides a browser, which you will need to surf the web, you will probably want to take advantage of e-mail as well. One of the original uses of the Internet, e-mail is still the most popular use.

E-mail is fast, convenient, and an inexpensive way to keep in touch with friends, relatives, and acquaintances all over the world. A good e-mail program will let you compose and send messages, receive and read messages, and even save and organize them.

The first time you use any e-mail program, you will have to "configure it" (set it up) to work with your ISP. You will need information from them to type into the e-mail program. Ask your ISP for the information you need.

For tips on using e-mail like a pro, see the *"Sending and Receiving E-Mail"* section.

Built-In Programs

Both Netscape Navigator and Internet Explorer come with an e-mail program built right in. Once you set it up properly, you will be able to click on an e-mail link within a Web page to send a message.

Separate Programs

Eudora Light is a popular e-mail program that works separately from your browser. It is free, and you can download it from `www.eudora.com`. The commercial version, Eudora Pro, is available for $30. It offers advanced features like message filtering (to automatically send junk mail to the trash, and kids' mail to their own mailboxes) and spell-checking.

ON THE WEB

Here are some other popular e-mail programs:

Pegasus Mail
www.pegasus.usa.com
Safe-Net Mail (Filters material deemed inappropriate for families
www.maiasoftware.com/safenet
Quick Mail
www.cesoft.com/quickmail/qmhome.html

Free E-Mail Accounts

Most ISPs give you an e-mail account as part of your online service. But there are many reasons you might wish to obtain a free e-mail account from another source:

- If you use a special e-mail account when you fill out forms or post messages to forums, you can divert junk mail away from your regular e-mail account.
- You can separate personal and business messages.
- Each member of the family can have a unique e-mail address.
- If you switch jobs or ISPs, your e-mail address will stay the same.
- If you don't have an account with an ISP (maybe you don't even have a computer). Even if you access the Internet through the library or Internet cafes, you can still use e-mail.

ON THE WEB

Here are some of the free, Web-based e-mail services:

Snap
www.e-mail.com

AltaVista E-mail
altavista.iname.com

HoTMail
www.hotmail.com

Lycos E-mail
e-mail.lycos.com/member/login.page

MailExcite
mailexcite.com

Pathfinder Mail
pathfinder.mail.com/member/login.page

Yahoo! Mail
mail.yahoo.com

Browsing The Web

Let's take a quick look at Internet Explorer, one of the browsers you might use to explore the Web.

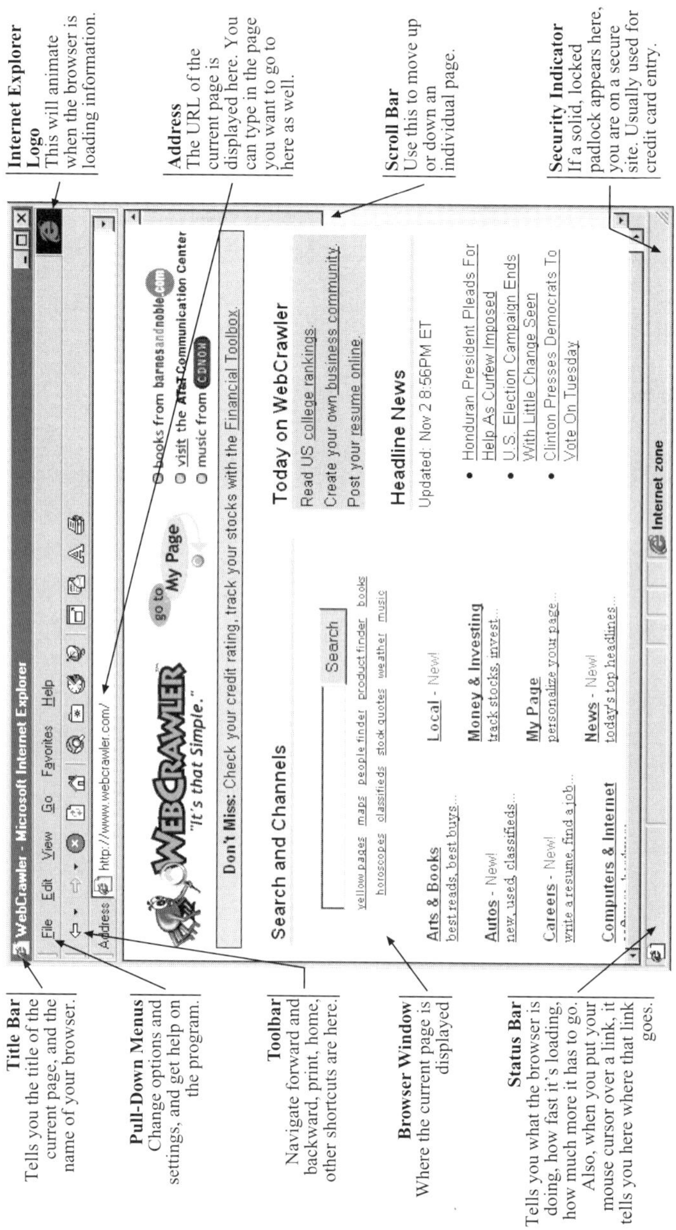

The toolbar contains shortcuts to a lot of the functions you will use most often. Let's take a look at the buttons on the toolbar, one by one:

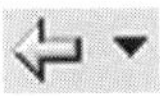 **Back and Next** 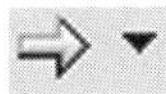

As you navigate the Web, moving from page to page, the browser keeps track of where you have been. Imagine you are dropping breadcrumbs in the woods. If you would like to return to a previous page (or even 10 pages back), click the Back button to follow the trail backwards. If you want to go forward along the trail, click the Forward button. Each time you click the Back or Forward buttons, the browser loads a new page. So be patient; wait to see what page comes up before you click again.

Both the Back and Next buttons have small, inverted triangles next to them. Click on the triangle to see a brief list of sites you have recently visited. Clicking any site name returns you to that site.

 **Stop**

Click this button to stop the browser from loading a Web page. If a page is taking too long to load, click the "Stop" button. Then try to load the page again, by clicking the "Refresh" button.

 **Refresh (or Reload)**

If a page changes often (for example, a page that displays stock quotes), your browser might be showing an outdated version of the page. Clicking the "Refresh" button forces the browser to show the latest version of the page.

 **Home (or Start)**

This brings you back to the first page you see whenever you first log on to the Web. You can decide what start page you would like to see; the *"Getting the Most Out of Your Browser"* section has step-by-step instructions. Since you can click on this button anytime to go back home, you will never get "lost."

Search

This button brings you to search engines, so you can find what you need. By default, this page will take you to a search page (Internet Explorer will take you to a Microsoft page; Navigator will take you to a Netscape page). You can set this button to take you to any search page you choose.

Favorites

Use this button to set a bookmark to a page you would like to return to later. Or, use it to return to a site you bookmarked previously. See the *"Getting Around on the Web"* section for tips on organizing your favorite bookmarks into categories.

History

Use this button to get a list of sites you have visited since the last time you logged in. Click on any site listed to return there.

Channels

This button brings up a list of sites who are "broadcasting" information (think of a network that broadcasts over a television channel). Usually, you will have to subscribe to a channel to see the information. Subscriptions are typically free.

Full Screen

Click this button to "maximize" your browser, so it takes up the entire desktop. This is recommended, so you can see more of every Web page.

Mail (and News)

Clicking this button brings up the built-in e-mail program and gives you access to Usenet newsgroups.

Print

Click this button to print the current Web page.

Getting Around On The Web

Getting around the Web (called navigating), is pretty simple once you get the hang of it. Let's go over some of the basics.

URL

Every Web page has its own address, called a URL. Take a look at the URL for this book:

`http://www.learntheweb.com`

URL stands for Uniform Resource Locator. Despite the fancy name, a URL works much like the address of a house or a business. Without it, people would not be able to find you. And you couldn't find anyone else.

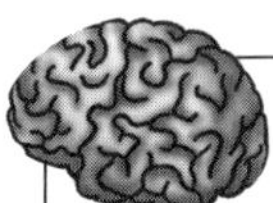

IMPRESS YOUR FRIENDS!

URLs might seem complicated, but it could be worse. A Web site address is actually a string of numbers and dots, like this: `207.53.24.108`. They are called IP addresses (short for Internet Protocol). Now, computers might not have any trouble remembering all those numbers, but humans sure do. So we came up with URLs, which are designed to make remembering these addresses a *little* easier.

Although many URLs look like a bunch of confusing symbols and letters, all those symbols do mean something. If you understand them, it will be easier for you to get where you're going on the Web. Let's break a URL down, so it will make more sense.

http://`www.learntheweb.com`

The first part of the URL tells you what type of information you are viewing. Most URLs will start with **http**, which indicates a Web page. In case you are curious, this stands for **HyperText Transfer Protocol**.

The http will always be followed by a colon and two forward slashes. On your keyboard, you can find the forward slash on the same key as the question mark.

http://**www**.learntheweb.com

The next part of the address is the computer where the Web site is located. A computer that **hosts** a Web site is called a **server**. The www stands for World Wide Web. This is the name of the server you'll be visiting. Not every server is called www, although it is the most common name. You might see other names, like home, as in home.netscape.com. Or sometimes you won't see any name at all.

http://www.**learntheweb.com**

Next comes the domain name. Here, learntheweb is the name of the site. .com is the **domain**, or the type of organization you are visiting (say the period before the com as "dot."). .com stands for Commercial, so most businesses have that domain. .com is the fastest growing domain, but there are others.

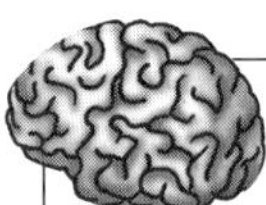

IMPRESS YOUR FRIENDS!

Here are some common domains:

.edu **= Education (Universities)**

.org **= Non-profit organizations**

.gov **= Government agencies**

.net **= Network**

.mil **= Military**

Some URLs are that simple. But others have another forward slash, and even more information. Think again about the address on a building. Remember, some addresses are more detailed. They have a room number, a department name, or the number of a floor in a building. URLs work the same way. If you see more information after the domain name, that means the address is pointing to a more specific place on the server.

http://www.learntheweb.com**/tutorial/urls.html**

Each word and forward slash in a URL stands for a directory. The last part of a URL you might see is the **file name**. This is the name of a particular web page, and it will usually end in `.html` or `.htm`. HTML stands for HyperText Markup Language. HTML is the language that web pages are written in.

If you know the URL of a Web site, you can just type it in the address (or location) box at the top of your browser. Then, press RETURN (or ENTER) on your keyboard, and the browser will take you there. Be careful to type in the URL exactly, with no spaces or misspellings - the browser is not at all forgiving when it comes to mistakes. If something is typed incorrectly, you will get a message telling you the site could not be found.

Of course, knowing the meaning behind the symbols does not make them any easier to type in. So, check the *"Getting the Most Out of Your Browser"* section for shortcuts.

Hyperlinks

The Web is made up of individual pages. A collection of pages is called a site. A link from one page to another page is called a hyperlink.

Words on a Web page can be hyperlinked to other pages. Often hyperlinked text is a different color than the rest of the text on the page (usually blue) and is underlined.

Pictures can be hyperlinks, too. Sometimes a picture will have a blue outline around it, letting you know it is a hyperlink. But often, Web site designers turn off the blue outline.

So how can you tell if text or pictures on a page are hyperlinks? Simply move your mouse cursor over the page. If your cursor changes to a pointing hand, then you have found a hyperlink. While your cursor is a hand, glance down at the status bar (in the lower left corner). It tells you where the link will take you.

One way to navigate the Web is to click on hyperlink after hyperlink to get where you want to go. Many sites have a list of "links" to other pages they think you might be interested in.

History Folder

Remember, the browser keeps track of every page you have visited in one session. If you would like to jump to any one of them, simply use the history folder. Here's how to do it:

Internet Explorer

Click the History button on the toolbar. A list of sites you have recently visited pops up on the left. You can sort them by the title of the site, the Internet address (URL), or the date you last visited the site. Click on any site title to instantly travel there. To hide the History, click the History button again.

Netscape Navigator

Click ⇨**History**. A list of sites you have recently visited pops up in a window. Double click on any site title to instantly travel there.

Favorites (Bookmarks)

Once you find a site you think you might want to visit again, set it as a Favorite. (If you are using Netscape Navigator, they are called Bookmarks.) Whenever you would like to return to that site, select it from the "Favorites" menu.

If you are using Explorer, choose **Favorites⇨Add to favorites...** The site currently in your browser window will be set as a favorite. The next time you would like to visit that site, return to the Favorites menu. Or, just click on the Favorites button on your toolbar. (For Netscape, use the "Bookmarks" menu.)

When you set a favorite, Explorer 4.0 will also give you the option of "subscribing" to the site. If you decide to subscribe, Explorer will automatically check the site for updates and download new pages to your hard drive. You can schedule a time for the updates (even in the middle of the night, when no one in the family needs the computer or the telephone line) and view the pages at your convenience. Be careful with subscriptions, however; the updates can eat up hard drive space rather quickly.

After a while, you may find that you have set so many bookmarks, your list is very long. It is easy to organize your favorite sites by category. In the Favorites menu, select "Organize Favorites." Make a new folder called "Travel," for example. You can move all the travel-related sites you have bookmarked to this folder. If you would like to remove a favorite, just click the site name once, and press DELETE, or click the **Delete** button.

Forms

Some Web sites ask you to fill out a form. A form may be required to register with a site, so you can explore the members-only sections. Or, you might order a product from an online store.

When you are on a page that contains a form, click somewhere inside the first box (called a field), and start typing. To jump to the next field, press the TAB key on your keyboard. If you need to back up a field, hold down the SHIFT key before you press TAB. Usually, at the end of the form, there will be a button that says "Submit." Click on this button to send in the form.

Be sure to read the *"Staying Smart, Safe, and Secure"* section before sending sensitive information like a Social Security number or a credit card number using a form.

Frames

Some Web sites organize themselves into frames, which means there are actually several pages on the screen at one time. Maximize your browser to see everything on the page (see the *"Getting the Most Out of Your Browser"* section on screen tips).

When Something Goes Wrong

Sites on the Web change all the time. A page that you look at one day might be gone the next. Sometimes your browser will tell you "Object Not Found," or "404 Error." That means the address in the browser's "Address" box was pointing to a spot on a server that cannot be found.

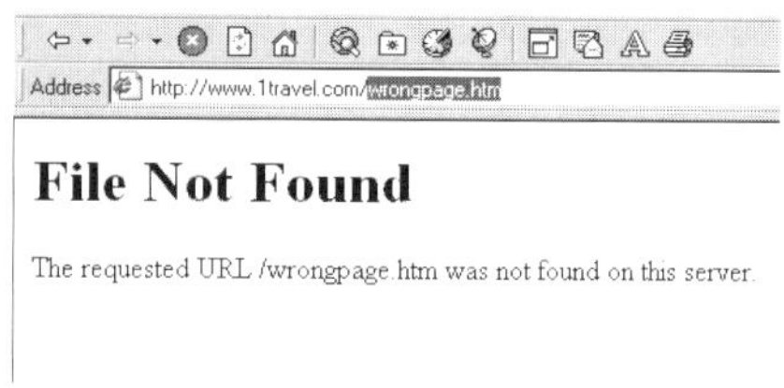

But there is still hope. Put your cursor in the Address box, and delete everything after the last forward slash. Usually, you will end up on a Web page that does exist, and you can find your way from there. If that still doesn't work, delete everything after the next to last forward slash. Keep going until you find a page that exists.

Getting the Most Out of Your Browser

Set Your Own Start Page

When you first log on to the Web, what do you see? Chances are you see Netscape's or Microsoft's default page. Or maybe your ISP has set up your Start page for you.

But you can choose any page you would like for your default start page. It's easy!

1) Choose your page

Before you choose a Start page, think about what you do when you are online. What kinds of sites do you visit often? When you log on to the Web, do you always go to the same place? Do you search for information or companies? Are you interested in information that changes frequently, like news, weather, sports scores, and stock quotes? Choose a start page that fits your interests.

ON THE WEB

Some Start page suggestions:

My Yahoo
`my.yahoo.com`

Search.com
`www.search.com`

Snap
`www.snap.com`

Cool Site of the Day
`www.coolsiteoftheday.com`

2) Set your page

Navigate to the Start page you would like to set.

Internet Explorer

Click **View⇨Internet Options**. Under the General tab, look for "Home Page." Click the "Use Current" button. Click "OK." The current page in your browser window is now your new Start page!

Netscape Navigator

Click **Edit⇨Preferences**. Click on the Navigator category. Under "Navigator starts with," select "Home Page." Under "Home Page," click the "Use Current Page." The current page in your browser window is now your new Start page!

3) Go home

When you first log on the Web, you will see your start page. Anytime during your Web surfing, click the "Home" button to return to this page.

Speed Up The Web

If you are wondering why the Web is so slow sometimes, refer to *Appendix B*. Keep reading this section for some tips to tune up your browser and speed up your surfing.

EXPERT ADVICE

How long should it take for a page to download? It depends on the speed of your modem. A 28.8K modem can download about 2 to 3 kilobytes per second. So, a 150K Web page should take about a minute.

Tip #1: Start with the right equipment

Use a PC that was produced in the last six months to one year. It should have enough memory and processor speed to handle Web surfing. You will need some free hard drive space to store files like graphics and video. Also, invest in the fastest modem you can afford. You will need at least a 28.8 Kbps modem, but faster is better.

Tip #2: Increase your cache size

Your cache is a temporary storage place where Web pages and graphics are stored. If you visit the same pages often, your browser can pull these files right from your local hard drive instead of from the Internet, saving you time. Check your browser settings to double or even triple your cache size:

Internet Explorer

Go to **View⇨Internet Options**. Under the "General" tab, look for "Temporary Internet Files". Click the "Settings..." button. To increase the number, point to the slider bar with your mouse cursor, hold your button down, and move the slider to the right. If you have enough free space on your hard drive, you can increase this to 10-15%. Click "OK."

Netscape Navigator

Click **Edit⇨Preferences...** Under the Advanced category, click on Cache. Next to "Disk Cache:" change the number in the field to a higher number (double or triple this number). Click "OK."

Be careful. The browser checks the entire cache before it downloads any new files. So if you travel to many different Web sites, increasing the cache too much will slow you down. In that case, lower your cache size and delete all temporary files in it (click on the "Clear Disk Cache Now" button).

Tip #3: Turn off the images

If you are looking for information and can do without the glitz, turn off the images.

Internet Explorer

Click **View⇨Internet Options**. Under "Multimedia", look for "Show Pictures". The box next to it should be checked. Click on it to uncheck the box. While you are there, uncheck "Play Animations", "Play Videos", and "Play Sounds" as well. Click "OK."

Netscape Navigator

Click **Edit⇨Preferences**. Click on the "Advanced" category. Click on "Automatically load images and other data types" until the box does not have an "X" in it. Click "OK."

If you are surfing the Web with image loading turned off, you can always load a particular image you would like to see. Point your mouse cursor to the space where the image would have been. Click the rightmost mouse button. From the menu that appears, select "Show picture." (On a Mac, hold down the CONTROL key and click on the image.)

Tip #4: Hang up and try again

If you are loading a Web page or downloading software, and a long time passes without much happening, you might not have a good connection with the server. Like a bad phone connection, you can always hang up and call right back. Click on the Stop button at the top of your browser, and try the link again. You will often find that a page that was taking a long time to load will now load instantly.

EXPERT ADVICE

Keep an eye on the Internet Explorer or Netscape Navigator logo at the top right corner of your browser. It will move when your browser is loading information. If it keeps moving for a long time (5 minutes or so) and nothing is happening on the page, stop the load and try again.

Tip #5: Avoid rush hour

By far, the busiest times on the Internet are between 2 and 4 in the afternoon, and 6 and 10 at night. Steer clear of the Web at those times if you can, unless you have a lot of patience.

When in doubt, you can always check the Internet Traffic Report before you go out, just to see how well the traffic is moving:

`www.internettrafficreport.com.`

ON THE WEB

You can try software to help speed up your experience. PeakJet is an accelerator, which automatically downloads the pages that link to the page you are looking at, anticipating your next click. It's $29.95 from Peak Technologies (`www.peak-media.com`) for Win95.

Surf Like A Pro

Here are a few more tips to help you get the most out of your browser:

Maximize Your Browser

A larger browser window means you can see more of the Web page, without scrolling. This will make it much easier to read the page. Try maximizing your browser so that it takes up the entire screen. You can do this by clicking on the Maximize button at the top right corner of the browser window (on a Windows 95 PC), or by dragging the bottom right corner of the window down and to the right (on a Macintosh).

Shrink the Toolbar

You can make the toolbar smaller, giving you more space in the browser window.

Internet Explorer

Click **View⇨Toolbars**. Uncheck "Text Labels".

You can get even more space by combining toolbars. Point your cursor to the "Links" or "Address" toolbars. By holding the mouse button down, you can move these toolbars up or down, combining them together.

Don't worry if you cannot see all the buttons at once; just double click on the word "Links" or "Address" to see the entire toolbar. Or, point your cursor at the two vertical lines to the left of each toolbar (your cursor will become an arrow) and hold your button down to move it left or right.

Netscape Navigator

Click **Edit⇨Preferences**. Click the "Appearance" tab. Under "Show Toolbar As," check "Pictures Only."

Turn off the security message

Your browser will warn you if you are about to do something potentially unsafe, like sending information to another computer (for example, when you fill out a form). These messages can get annoying after awhile. As long as you are following the safety tips explained in the *"Staying Smart, Safe, and Secure"* section, you can turn them off.

Internet Explorer

Click **View⇨Internet Options**. Click the "Security" tab. Select **Medium** or **Low** security.

Netscape Navigator

 ⇨**Security Info**. Click "Navigator." Under "Show a warning before:" uncheck "Sending unencrypted information to a site."

Change Your Font Size

If words on a Web page are too small or too large for comfortable reading, they can be adjusted.

Microsoft Explorer

Click **View⇨Fonts⇨Largest to Smallest**.

Netscape Navigator

Click **Edit⇨Preferences**. Under the "Appearance" tab, select "Fonts." For both "Variable" and "Fixed Width Font," select a larger or smaller size.

Save Images

With a PC, right click on any image in a Web page to save it on your hard drive (only for personal use – don't violate any copyright laws!) You can also set any image as your desktop wallpaper, by selecting that choice from the menu that appears. (On a Mac, hold down the `CONTROL` key and click on the image.)

Copy Text

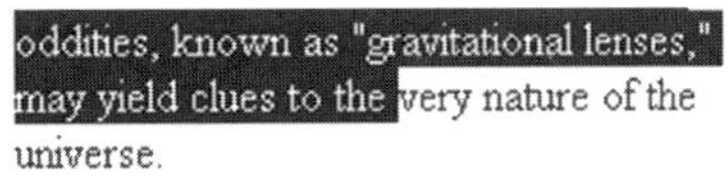

To copy text from a Web page, highlight the text — point the mouse cursor at the beginning of the text passage, hold the left mouse button down, move the cursor to the end of the passage, and release the button. Click the Edit menu, and select "Copy."

Next, open your favorite word processor (like Windows Wordpad or Notepad). Click the Edit menu in your word processor, and select "Paste." (This trick can be useful if you are having trouble printing the Web page from your browser. You will be able to print it from your favorite word processor.)

Take A Look Back

On a PC, right click on the Back or Forward button for a short list of recently visited sites. (On a Mac, hold down the CONTROL key before you click.)

For more tips and help, turn to the Web:

Microsoft Explorer

www.microsoft.com/IESupport

Netscape Navigator

help.netscape.com

PART II:

Getting the Hang of It

In this section, you will discover how to:

- find whatever you are looking for on the Web
- send and receive e-mail
- use proper e-mail etiquette
- download software
- create your own Web site

Stop Searching - Find What You Want

The World Wide Web is huge. Millions of sites contain billions of pages. The Web has been doubling in size every 100 days. Sites appear and disappear daily. And, there is no handy directory to help you find your way around. So finding just the information you need can be like searching for a needle in 150 million haystacks spread across more than 50 countries

This section will give you the tips you need to find anything you are looking for.

Try The Obvious

URLs for companies generally follow the same format: www, then a dot, then the company name (no spaces, punctuation, or capital letters), then another dot, then com. So for example, if you are looking for Apple's Web site, just type in:

`www.apple.com`

Simple, right?

Remember, you will use `.com` for a company, `.org` for a non-profit agency, `.gov` for a government agency, and `.edu` for a university. So, typing in

EXPERT ADVICE

If you are using Netscape or Internet Explorer 4.0, here's an easy trick. In the "Location" ("Address") box, type in the name of the company whose site you are looking for. (This works especially well for a large company with a short name, like UPS.) Press `ENTER` (`RETURN`) on your keyboard. You will be taken to `www.ups.com`, if it exists. Since most large companies follow this format for their Web site addresses, this method works fairly often.

```
www.greenpeace.org
```

will take you right to the Greenpeace site. And, typing

```
www.lsu.edu
```

will take you to ... well, you get the idea.

"Find" A Site Easily

If you are having trouble finding the site, there is a trick built into Internet Explorer that can help. In the "Address" box, type the word "find" and a keyword or two. Explorer will bring you to Yahoo!, where it will hopefully list the site you are looking for. Click on the link, and you are off. This time, you can use spaces if you like. For example, typing in

```
find american airlines
```

will give you will give you a short list of sites, including the American Airlines home page. You can also put phrases in quotes to help narrow down your search. For example, typing in

```
find "state farm insurance"
```

will give you only three links to look through, rather than the 15 or more you would get if you did not use quotation marks.

Directory Assistance

In a library, you would use the card catalog for a complete, organized directory of every book the library holds. This makes it easy to find a particular book. And, there is always a helpful librarian available who can assist you in your search.

The Web, unfortunately, does not have a card catalog. There is no helpful librarian. Plus, the Web changes constantly. Web sites appear, disappear, and change every day. There is no central location for sites to register what subject they cover and how recently they have been updated.

Some Web sites, called **directories**, try to list as many sites as possible. They can be a great place to start your search. A directory lists Web sites in categories, similar to the phone directory. You can browse by category, or search the listings for a particular word. Yahoo is a very popular directory:

> ***Yahoo!***
> www.yahoo.com

Yahoo is the largest and most comprehensive of the Web directories. Yahoo's categories are a great place to browse for a site when you are just not sure what to look for. With categories like Business, Reference, Entertainment, and Sports, there is a place for just about any kind of site. There is even a regional section, with a category devoted to New Orleans-related sites.

ON THE WEB

Other Directories to Try:

> ***Lycos Top 5%:***
> point.lycos.com/categories
> ***The Mining Company:***
> www.miningco.com
> ***Magellan:***
> www.mckinley.com

Keep in mind that most directories rely on humans to update their listings. It would be impossible for them to list every site that exists on the Web at any one time. So if a directory doesn't have what you need, don't give up. You can always try a search engine instead.

Try a Search Engine

Search engines are very powerful tools that attempt the impossible: they try to provide you with a way to find any word on any page in the world. They do this by using automated software agents, called "spiders," which crawl from site to site, cataloging what they find in huge databases. Alta Vista is one very powerful search engine:

Alta Vista
`www.altavista.digital.com`

Digital Equipment Corporation's search engine, Alta Vista, is probably the most powerful search engine at this time, with a database of over 125 million Web pages.

Alta Vista is a great tool if you are looking for something that may not have a whole site dedicated to it, but may be mentioned somewhere on a page. For instance, searching for "Audrey Hepburn" will turn up over 7,700 matches, on topics ranging from her movie history, to dolls and posters for sale, to trivia and photos. Alta Vista will find your keywords on any page in its database, in whatever context the keywords are mentioned.

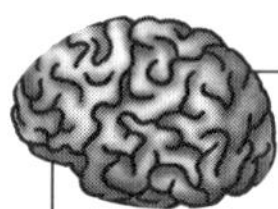

IMPRESS YOUR FRIENDS!

To have some fun with a search engine, try "ego surfing." Type your own name into the search engine to see where it appears. You might be surprised!

EXPERT ADVICE

Alta Vista will let you know how popular your site is. Typing in `link:yoursite.com` **will return everyone that hyperlinks to a page somewhere on your site. To leave out pages within your own site that link to each other, type the command like this:**

```
link:yoursite.com -host:yoursite.com
```

ON THE WEB

Other Search Engines To Try:

InfoSeek: `www.infoseek.com`

HotBot: `www.hotbot.com`

Excite: `www.excite.com`

Lycos: `www.lycos.com`

Which to Choose?

A directory is the place to start if you are looking for a company's site or you need general information. If you are searching for more obscure information or you want to do an exhaustive search, use a search engine.

Yahoo will search for your keywords first in its own directory. Then it will pass your keywords on to a search engine for a more thorough search. For most of the information you will probably look for, this will be the best place to start. See the *"Finding What You Want"* section for tips on improving your search results.

Alternative Searches

Search Everywhere at Once

For an extremely thorough search on a topic, you can use a **metasearch** to look in several databases at once. SavvySearch, a tool at Colorado State University, will send your query to 23 databases simultaneously, and give you the results from all of them. The address is a bit unusual:

`guaraldi.cs.colostate.edu:2000`.

Another metasearch tool, Internet Sleuth (`www.isleuth.com`), will allow you to send your query to six search engines simultaneously. The Internet Sleuth site is also an excellent resource for finding specialized information, as it includes hundreds of databases. You can search through the complete texts of Shakespeare, Chaucer, and even Dr. Suess, or find out what to feed your pet scorpion. Internet Sleuth gives you an easy way to search for news, software, books and CDs, magazines, and more.

Searching for a Search Engine

With all these different search engines and directories, it was only a matter of time before someone created a directory of directories, right? That is exactly what you will find at C|Net's Search.com (`www.search.com`). The search engines themselves are listed in categories like Automotive, Health, Shopping, and Travel. Where else can you find a search engine devoted to golf courses?

Get Your Questions Answered

Okay, the Internet does not have a librarian. But it does have a virtual librarian, and his name is Jeeves. Jeeves is the personal automated Web research assistant at Ask Jeeves (www.askjeeves.com). Start by asking him a question. He will come back with questions for you, to clarify what you want to know. Then he will present you with one site, which should answer your question.

ON THE WEB

You can "peek behind the curtain" to see what other people are asking Jeeves. Here are some actual questions:

Where can I learn English slang?

Why is the sky blue?

What is the diameter of Jupiter?

Are certain people more prone to stress?

Am I in love?

What should I name my baby?

How much should I weigh?

Where is The Bureau of Missing Socks?

Kids Only!

There are some directories devoted to kids sites. These can be great places to find safe, kid-friendly content. See the *"Take a Guided Tour of the Web: Kids"* section for a list.

Find A Long Lost Friend

Specialty search engines are available to help you find e-mail addresses, postal addresses, telephone numbers, and personal Web sites. See the *"Guided Tour: People"* section for a list of sites.

Eavesdropping for Answers

Chances are your question has already been asked (and answered!) within Usenet, (the Internet newsgroups). A very unique search engine, DejaNews (`www.dejanews.com`) gives you the power to search Usenet messages.

Software

Don't search for shareware and freeware using a regular search engine; use an archive. See the *"Guided Tour: Computers & Technology"* section.

Find A Job

Many sites offer databases filled with thousands of jobs you can search through. See the *"Guided Tour: Career & Money"* section.

News Search Engines

Use a specialty news search engine to look for the latest headlines. See the *"Guided Tour: News & Weather"* section.

Tips For Better Searches

1. Use the Right Tool

Remember, every search engine and directory is different and will give you different results. If you type a common word like `skydiving` into a search engine, you will have to sift through thousands of pages. Better to start with a directory. On the other hand, typing `Aaron Copeland` into a directory might not get great results; you are better off using a search engine. And if you are looking for specialized information (like real estate or job listings), use a specialty search whenever possible.

2. Use Keywords

Keywords are unique words that help a search engine know what you are looking for. The opposite would be a stopword - a word so common, it appears everywhere. Search engines ignore **stopwords**, so avoid using them.

Here are some common stopwords:

a	**is**	**if**	**in**	**the**	**but**	**with**
I	**it**	**we**	**for**	**you**	**any**	**about**

3. Boolean Operators

Using Boolean operators sounds more complicated than it is. When search engines talk about Boolean operators, they are referring to the words AND and OR. Using AND between two keywords tells the search engine to look for pages that contain both of the words. Using OR between two words says to look for pages that contain **either** keyword.

For example, if you are looking for recipes with ginger, typing in `ginger recipe` will give you everything from the Spice Girls to Ginger of Gilligan's Island. To narrow your search, type in `ginger AND recipe`.

```
hurricane AND rum
beans AND rice
xfiles OR x-files
Mardi Gras OR Fat Tuesday
```

4. Plus and Minus

Related to Boolean operators are the operators `+` and `-`. They can be used to exclude and require words. For example, if you are researching historical documents about the Titanic, and you want to avoid Leonardo DiCaprio fan club sites, try typing in `+Titanic +history -movie`.

5. Pick A Favorite

If there is a search engine you use fairly often, take some time to read its "*Tips*" section. All search engines are a little different, so reading the tips will help you get the most out of your searches.

6. Check Your Spelling

Search engines, like browsers, are unforgiving when it comes to spelling. If you don't spell your keywords exactly right, you may be very disappointed in the results. When in doubt and without a dictionary, type your keywords into software that has a built-in spell checker (like a word processor or an e-mail program) and check them.

7. Be Unique

Type in a word like `baseball` into most search engines, and you will get millions of pages to sift through. But type in `New Orleans Zephyrs` and you will get a few hundred. Try to use unique, specific terms whenever you can to narrow down your search.

8. Terms of a Feather Should Flock Together

Surround phrases with quotation marks. Searching for the keywords `shotgun` and `house` will return millions of pages, covering every topic from gun control to the House of Representatives. Putting the phrase in quotation marks will really narrow your search.

9. Add a Wildcard

Use the asterisk symbol (*) in place of some of the letters in a word. This is helpful if you are looking for a word that has alternate spellings. For example, typing in the keyword `theat*` will find the words theater and theatre.

Sending And Receiving E-Mail

E-mail is about the fastest, easiest, and cheapest way for people to keep in touch, no matter how far away they may be. Families are discovering how to use e-mail to keep in touch with far-flung relatives. Businesses are using it to keep their employees communicating, whether it is across the hallway or across the ocean. Even if your friends and family are close to home, e-mail can be a very convenient way to broadcast a message to a whole group of people at once, like party plans or an announcement of good news.

Anatomy of an E-Mail Address

Most e-mail addresses look basically the same. They all start with a user name:

snoopy@doghouse.com

The user name might be a last name, a first name, or both. It might be a nickname. Or it could be a number. If you can choose your own user name, choose a name that is easy for other people to remember, like your first name.

The username is followed by the "at" sign:

snoopy**@**doghouse.com

The @ separates the user name from the rest of the address. If you look on your keyboard, you will see the "at" sign just above the number 2.

The last part of an e-mail address is the domain name:

snoopy@**doghouse.com**

The domain name is the location of the computer where your e-mail is delivered. This might be the name of your company or of your Internet Service Provider (ISP). For example, if you are an America Online subscriber, your domain name will be `aol.com`. Remember, only companies have domains that end in `.com`. Universities end in `.edu`, government agencies end in `.gov`, and network domains end in `.net`.

The Basics

To send an e-mail to someone, all you need is their e-mail address. Just like a postal letter, an e-mail has to be addressed correctly to reach its destination. In the "To:" field, type the e-mail address very carefully. If you would like to send the same message to more than one person, type a comma after the first address, then add the second address. You can add as many addresses as you would like; just add a comma before each address. (Note: Some e-mail programs use a semi-colon instead of a comma.)

EXPERT ADVICE

Save A Tree

One of the purposes of e-mail is to cut down on the amount of paper companies use. But many people print every e-mail message they receive.

You can save a lot of paper and ink, and still save important messages, by filing them in your e-mail program. Most e-mail programs have a system for organizing and saving important messages. For example, Eudora has "folders". You can make a new folder, name it anything you want, and transfer messages from your in-box to the new folder. Open the folder any-time to review your messages.

Before you send it, type a few words saying what the message is about in the "Subject:" field. If your message is very important and time-sensitive, starting your subject with "URGENT" will get attention. Just don't overuse this.

If you would like to send a copy of the message to someone else, type their address in the "CC:" (Carbon Copy) field. Most e-mail programs also have a "BCC:" (Blind Carbon

Copy) field as well. Use this field if you would like to send a copy to someone without the first recipient knowing. Then type your message. When you are finished, click on the "Send" button, and off it goes!

The message is sent to your Internet Service Provider (assuming you are connected and everything is configured correctly; see the *"How Do I Get Online"* section). From there, your message is forwarded to the Internet, where it is sent on to the recipient's ISP. The message stays there, on the ISP's server, until the recipient checks her e-mail. Then the server sends the message to the recipient's computer.

E-mail is such a new and unique way for people to communicate, it has its own etiquette and customs. It is important to be aware of the Do's and Don'ts of e-mail: you can avoid misunderstandings and get your message across without offending anyone.

In fact, a whole new word has been coined to describe proper e-mail behavior: netiquette. Short for "Internet Etiquette," netiquette means much more than just "being polite." The rules of netiquette help avoid misunderstandings and go a long way toward keeping the peace in Cyberspace. Before you send another e-mail message, read the next section.

Netiquette

E-mail tends to be more casual then a letter. People use a writing style that is conversational; more like a phone call.

Of course, in a phone call or a face-to-face conversation, you don't depend on words alone to get your message across. Imagine you are talking to an old friend. Your friend hears your tone of voice, sees the expressions on your face, even watches your body language. So if you are joking, or being sarcastic, he can usually tell. And, if you say something that offends him, you will be able to tell by the expression on his face. You will be able to adjust your words or your tone of voice.

With e-mail, your friend cannot see your face or hear your voice. He must rely on the words you use to understand what you mean. You must be very careful about what you say, so that you are not misunderstood.

Often, you are sending messages to business associates or even strangers. Since they do not know you like your old friend does, you must be even more careful about what you say. You cannot assume anything about their nationality, gender, age, or even their mood.

Read on for some tips to help you get your message across.

Emphasis

Emphasizing a certain word in a sentence can change the whole meaning of a sentence. You can add light emphasis to a word by surrounding it with asterisks:

```
Is there *any* movie you haven't seen
yet?
```

For strong emphasis, use capital letters and exclamation points:

```
If I don't finish that report tonight
I'll be in BIG TROUBLE!!!
```

BUT - and this is important - use capital letters sparingly. Why? Read on:

PLEASE DON'T YELL

Don't overuse capital letters. One of the most important netiquette rule is to turn off the "Caps Lock" key. WHEN YOU TYPE IN CAPITAL LETTERS, PEOPLE THINK YOU ARE SHOUTING AT THEM. Most of the time, writing an entire sentence in capital letters is overkill:

```
I AM FINE THANK YOU. HOW ARE YOU DOING?
```

Capital letters, besides being considered rude, are harder to read than mixed-case letters. Avoid typing entire messages in capitals. If, for some reason, you cannot type in mixed case, choose all lower case letters instead:

```
Unless your message is vitally impor-
tant, mixed case is better. or even
lower case is ok.
```

Creative Punctuation

Question marks, exclamation points, and other punctuation can also help get your message across. As mentioned before, exclamation points can help add emphasis to what you are saying. Similarly, more than one question mark in a row can help convey the fact that you are really curious:

```
So, what are you getting me for my
birthday????
```

Used together, question marks and exclamation points can mean surprise, shock, or dismay:

```
?!?Why didn't you tell me that yester-
day??!!?
```

A string of punctuation can, of course, stand for something that would be too impolite to type:

```
My &$#%#$* computer keeps crashing!!
```

(Of course, like capital letters, punctuation should not be overused either.)

Emoticons

Emoticons stand for "emotional icons." They are symbols used as shortcuts in e-mail. You might have seen one before:

```
:-)
```

Emoticons are sometimes called smileys. If you don't understand why, tilt your head to the left and look at it again.

IMPRESS YOUR FRIENDS!

Some of the most common emoticons:

:-) **Smiley face**

;-) **Wink (light sarcasm)**

:-(**Frown (anger or displeasure)**

:-@ **Scream**

Since your reader cannot hear your tone of voice or see your facial expressions, emoticons can be very useful when you want to let someone know that you are being sarcastic, or teasing, or upset

```
Did you want to treat me to lunch
today? ;-)
```

For a list of smileys , see the *Glossary*.

Acronyms

Because e-mail is meant to be fast and save time, many people rely on acronyms as a shorthand. You will also see acronyms in newsgroups, chat rooms, and bulletin boards. Some common acronyms are BTW (By The Way), IMHO (In My Humble Opinion), and LOL (Laughing Out Loud).

```
That joke you sent yesterday had me
LOL.
```

IMPRESS YOUR FRIENDS!

A few more common acronyms:

FWIW **For What It's Worth**

FYI **For Your Information**

ROTFL **Rolling On The Floor Laughing**

TTFN **Ta Ta For Now**

TTYL **Talk To You Later**

See the *Glossary* for a list of acronyms you will probably see.

Replying

Although e-mail is delivered quickly, the reply may not necessarily be immediate. So it is usually preferable to repeat (quote) some of the message back in your reply. For instance, instead of answering:

```
Yes
```

Instead, answer:

```
>Can you meet for lunch this Friday?

Yes
```

In the above example, the quote from the original message starts with ">." This is intended to set apart your reply. Most e-mail programs will add the ">" for you automatically when you click the "Reply" button.

If the message you are responding to is very long, don't quote the entire message in your reply. You can quote only the part of the message that is relevant, and leave out plenty in between. It is considered wasteful to quote a very long message for a one-sentence reply. You can show that you edited out parts of the message with an ellipse:

```
>And when I woke up this morning

...

>so I didn't even realize it until din-
nertime!

Wow! That's quite a story!
```

They may then reply to your reply:

```
>>Can you meet for lunch this Friday?

>Yes

Great. How about 11:30?
```

Grammar

E-mail is more similar to a conversation than to a letter or a report. So people tend to be more casual and sloppier with the rules of grammar.

But when you send an e-mail, it represents you, so you probably want to make a good impression. It is a good idea to spell everything correctly, especially if you are sending a message to your boss or to a client. Of course, there is no reason to pull out your high school grammar textbook if you are sending a message asking where everyone is meeting for margaritas after work.

Time Out

The great thing about e-mail is when you click the "Send" button, your message rushes across the Internet to someone else's computer. The unfortunate thing about e-mail is that once you click the "Send" button, your message is gone. You cannot change your mind and take it back.

There have been many times when a click of the mouse has sent the wrong message, sometimes to many people. To avoid embarrassing mistakes, take a minute before you click the "Send" button to re-read your message. Make sure what you have written cannot be easily misunderstood.

If you are sending a message in anger, take this a step further. Before you send the message, take five. Go get some coffee, or just walk outside for a minute. When you return, read your message again. If you still feel like sending the message as is, go ahead.

ON THE WEB

For more about e-mail netiquette, try these sites:

May Houten-Kemp's Everything E-mail:
`everythingemail.net`

The Mining Company's Guide to E-mail:
`e-mail.miningco.com`

A Beginner's Guide to Effective E-Mail:
`www.webfoot.com/advice/e-mail.top.html`

Security

E-mail is about as private as a cellular phone conversation. Which is to say, it is not necessarily private at all. It is not difficult for other people, with the right know-how, to read what you think is a private message. Don't say anything in e-mail at work that you would not want your boss to read. Don't e-mail sensitive information that you would not want your competitors to know. Don't send credit card numbers or other important information over e-mail.

Remember that e-mail, once you send it, travels from your computer, to your ISP's computer, through several other computers on the Internet, to your recipient's ISP's computer, to its final destination. At each stop along the way, the message can be intercepted and read. Also, many ISPs make frequent back-up copies of the information on their computers. If your message is backed up, it will be saved for some period of time, maybe even years. There have been cases where, in a lawsuit, old e-mail messages that people thought were long deleted have been recovered by attorneys.

In addition, many companies deliberately (and legally) keep copies of employees' e-mail messages. A company can review these messages for any reason. Many employees don't worry about this, since their e-mail accounts are password-protected. But the system administrator at a company can usually access any e-mail account. Be especially careful about sending offensive or off-color jokes, since they may be used against you later.

There are ways to make e-mail more secure; see the *"Staying Smart, Safe, and Secure"* section.

You've Got Spam

Believe it or not, you are bound to start getting junk e-mail. Unsolicited, bulk e-mail is called **spam**. The name comes from a classic Monty Python skit set in a restaurant, where every dish on the menu came with Spam.

The practice of spamming, or sending junk e-mail to thousands of e-mail addresses at once, is causing a lot of controversy. (Spamming can also refer to posting messages to Usenet that have nothing to do with the topic being discussed.) Spamming is considered bad netiquette, and many ISPs have policies against their customers sending it.

But companies (and individuals) persist. Unlike regular junk mail delivered via the postal service, junk e-mail costs little or nothing to send. There is no postage and no printing cost. It is cheap and easy to send.

Why is spam so bad? Because, unlike regular junk mail, junk e-mail costs everyone else money. It wastes Internet bandwidth. It uses space on ISP servers, which increases their cost of doing business (and increases the cost of your Internet access). It takes up space on a company's server. It is time consuming for employees to read through and delete spam. Sometimes, you may receive so much spam, it can be difficult to find the real messages.

Most legitimate businesses will not send you e-mail announcements unless you request them by filling out a form at their Web site. They will often say in the message that you can remove yourself from the mailing list by replying to the message and typing "Remove" in the subject line. But be careful. Often, a spammer will trick you into replying to a message this way. Once you do, the spammer knows your address is legitimate, and will send you even more messages.

How do spammers get your e-mail address? Spammers collect the e-mail addresses of people who post messages to Usenet or on bulletin boards. Some companies collect your address on forms you fill out at their Web sites and sell their mailing lists to other companies. Some spammers use the America Online profiles that users fill out. Some chain e-mails or fake virus warnings are really tricks to collect the e-mail addresses of you and all of the people you forward the message to.

Here are some tips to avoid spam:

1. Many e-mail programs can be configured to filter out spam for you. SpammerSlammer (`www.spammerslammer.com`) is freeware that works with your e-mail software. SpammerSlammer scans incoming e-mail messages for common subject lines, return addresses from known offenders, and other warning signs, and transfers spam to the trash. If a message is doubtful, it is sent to a special mailbox, where you can review it before sending it to the trash.

2. When you receive spam, you can try to complain to their ISP. Take the address of the message, and replace the user name with postmaster. For example, if the message was sent from `joe@acme.com`, send a message to `postmaster@acme.com`. Include a copy of the entire e-mail, and tell them you do not wish to receive any more unsolicited e-mail from this account. If the ISP receives enough complaints, they may cancel the spammer's account. (Unfortunately, many spammers use forged return e-mail addresses, so this doesn't always work.)

3. If you often post to Usenet or bulletin boards, use an e-mail address that is different than your primary address. Many Web sites offer free e-mail accounts for your use (see *"Sending and Receiving E-mail"*). Dejanews (`www.dejanews.com`), a site which lets you read and post to Usenet, offers free, spam-filtered e-mail accounts.

Signatures

Unlike a letter, it is not possible to physically sign your e-mail. People often use electronic signatures to sign their messages.

Signatures for business messages typically contain your full name, your company name and your title, and your return e-mail address. Personal signatures can get pretty creative. Some people include a favorite quote. Others draw pictures with keyboard characters.

```
             (O O)
 +-oOO----(_)----------+
 |     Dr. Jeff Gettler   |
 |      (504) 555-1212    |
 +-----------------oOO--+
          |__|__|
           ||  ||
          oOO  Ooo
```

Don't go overboard with your signature. In general, it is considered rude to have a signature that is longer than your actual message. A good rule of thumb is to keep your signature under 5 lines.

Many e-mail programs will let you type a signature to use. Or you can specify a file to use, if you want to get more elaborate. First, create a signature with any text editor (like Notepad for Windows users). Save the signature file as a plain text (`.txt`) file. Once you set up the signature, it will automatically appear at the bottom of every message you send.

ON THE WEB

If you need inspiration for your signature:

Bartlett's Familiar Quotations:
www.columbia.edu/acis/bartleby/bartlett

Coolsig:
www.coolsig.com

The Signature Museum:
huizen.dds.nl/~mwpieter/sigs

Attachments

Sometimes, you might want to send more than a plain text message via e-mail. For example, if you are inviting people to a gathering at your house, you might want to include a map. You can attach any type of file to an e-mail message, from a picture to a software program.

With most e-mail programs, you would click on a "paper clip" button to attach a file to a message.

Your e-mail program will encode (pack up) the file to send across the Internet. On the other end, your recipient's e-mail program will decode (unpack) the file. This is automatic, and you usually will not even be aware that it is happening.

EXPERT ADVICE

Do not confuse the encoding of an attachment with security. Anyone can still read the message, since it is automatically decoded at the other end.

When you receive an attachment via e-mail, you will need to know where it was stored. Look in the settings of your e-mail program to determine where attachments are saved. It might be a good idea to create an attachments folder on your desktop and have all of your attachments saved there.

Mailing Lists

Once you have an e-mail account, you can join a mailing list. A mailing list is a group of people who receive e-mail on a particular topic. Sometimes, members of a mailing list might receive a newsletter, sent by someone monthly, weekly, or even daily. Some mailing lists are like newsgroups or bulletin boards, where the subscribers to the list can send messages to the group, and ask questions. The messages are all consolidated into one e-mail and sent to everyone on the list.

Usually, you can subscribe to a mailing list by sending an e-mail to the list master. You will then get timely information and updates delivered right to your desktop. Most newsletters are free and are sent to you until you unsubscribe.

Mailing lists exist for every topic you can imagine, from technology to religion. The largest mailing list is C|Net's Digital Dispatch (`www.cnet.com/Community/Welcome/Dispatch`), with almost 900,000 subscribers. The Digital Dispatch is a weekly newsletter, containing summaries of C|Net's latest technology stories.

To find a mailing list that you would like to join, visit Reference.com (`www.reference.com`). They maintain a list of lists - hundreds of mailing lists on topics as diverse as "Angels" to "Administering 10K Road Races."

ON THE WEB

PC World magazine offers several newsletters (www.pcworld.com/resources/tipaday/tipsjoin.html**), including the "Windows 95 Tip of the Day," and the "Daily Virus Alert." Check off as many as you like, and they will be sent to you free of charge.**

"This is True" (www.thisistrue.com**), contains bizarre and true stories. Weird news stories and dumb criminal stories are sent right to your e-mailbox.**

Have a Virtually Nice Day

Another fun use of e-mail is virtual greetings. Many sites offer a virtual greeting card or post card that you can send, free of charge. Some cards are animated, or play music. And, most can be personalized with a message.

ON THE WEB

Try These:

Internet Card Central:
www.cardcentral.net

Blue Mountain Arts:
www.bluemountainarts.com

CyberPanda Best 100 of Virtual Greetings:
www.cyberpanda.com/postcard/best.shtml

Downloading Software

What is downloading?

To download is to copy software from a computer on the Internet to your own computer. Downloading is very simple to learn. Once you feel comfortable downloading, you can take advantage of a wealth of free software available on the Web. There are thousands of programs available - games, screen savers, useful utilities, business software, clip art, software for home and gardens, hobbies, even plug-ins for your browser.

How long does downloading take?

The time it takes to download a file depends on four factors:

1. The size of the file
2. The speed of your modem
3. The traffic conditions on the Internet
4. The speed of the computer from which you are downloading the file (called the FTP server)

#1 and #2 are easy to determine and can give you a good idea of how long it should take to download a file under ideal conditions. You can expect a 56 Kbps modem to take at least 3 minutes for every 1 megabyte in the file. So, a 5-megabyte file will take 15 minutes (or more) to download. (A 28.8 Kbps modem will take twice as long, or 6 minutes per every 1 megabyte.)

#3 varies quite a bit. If there is a lot of traffic on the Internet, your download will be slower. To understand why, remember how much slower you have to drive on the highway during rush hour. With all the other cars in the way, it takes much longer to travel even a short distance. Internet traffic affects how quickly your file can download in much the same way. The amount of traffic on the Internet might change dramatically by the hour. For tips on avoiding the Internet rush hour, see the *"Getting the Most Out of Your Browser"* section.

#4 varies also. Just as your modem has a set speed at which it can transfer information (28.8 Kbps, 56 Kbps, or other speeds), the FTP server has a speed as well. If the server has a slower connection to the Internet, your download will be slower. Plus, the server may be responding to several other people at the same time. If many people are trying to download files at the same time from this server, your download will be slower. (To avoid this, just try your download again later in the day.)

When you start your download, most browsers will let you know how much more time the download will take with a "progress indicator." In the beginning of the download, the estimate might be way off base; as the transfer continues, the estimate will be much more accurate.

Is downloading safe?

The main concern people have with downloading software from the Internet is that their computer will catch a virus. Actually, any software you install on your computer (including commercial software bought in a store) might be infected with a virus. There are three steps you can take to protect yourself:

1) **Buy (and use) anti-virus software.** (See *"Staying Smart, Safe, and Secure."*)

2) **Only download software from reputable sites.** Before you download from an unfamiliar site, take some time to look around. If you get a good impression of the site and the kind of people who run it, then you should be safe. Most of the larger software archives, like `www.software.com` and `www.hotfiles.com`, scan all software for viruses before making it available for you to download.

3) **Back up your data.** It is a good idea to make backup copies of important files on your hard drive, since a number of things can go wrong with your system. Besides viruses, there are system crashes, physical damage to your computer, or accidental

erasures. When you are deciding which files to back up, think of the files you could not replace if something happened. Commercial software that you purchased and installed from floppy disks or CD-ROMs can be easily reinstalled. But the great American novel you have been writing, or your financial data, cannot easily be replaced. Make a copy now, before you have any problems, and remind yourself to back up regularly.

Going for it - downloading

Usually the site will have a hyperlink that says, "Download now." Click on that link to initiate the download. (If only everything was that simple!)

Next, your browser will ask you what you want to do with the file - open it or save it to disk. Select "Save to disk."

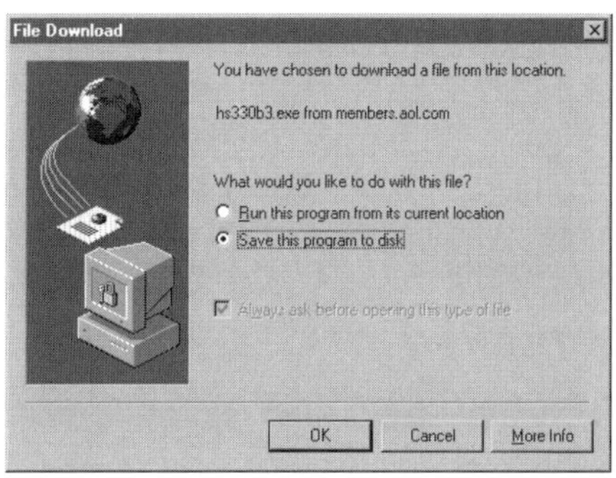

You will then be asked where you would like to save the file. This is probably the most important part of the download, since this is the point at which most people get very confused. It does not matter where you save the file. What matters is that you **remember where the file has been saved**. The easiest choice is to save the file to your desktop.

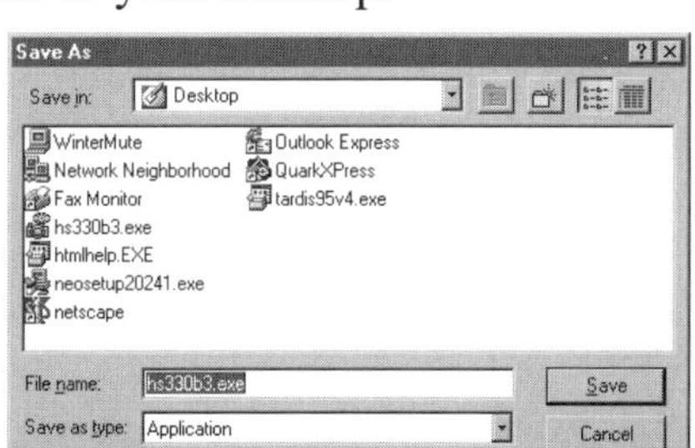

A name for the file will automatically be suggested. You can change the name if you would like, but it is not necessary.

When the "Saving file" box disappears, minimize your browser (click on the small button at the top left corner of your browser - the button that has a minus sign on it). You should see the file on your desktop. If you saved the file somewhere else (for example, in a folder), use Windows Explorer to find it.

Two types of files

What you will do next depends on what type of file you just downloaded. Some are self-extracting, and some are zipped.

Self-extracting

A self-extracting file is the easiest type of file to handle. Self-extracting files generally end with the extension `.exe`. With your left mouse button, double click on the file. It will automatically decompress and begin a simple installation program. Follow the directions on screen. At the end of the installation, a message will display, announcing the installation is complete.

Next, look for the installed program. It might be a new file on your desktop (besides the file you downloaded earlier). Or, it might be a new shortcut in your "Start" menu.

The original file you downloaded can be discarded now. Drag it to the recycle bin. You won't need it anymore.

Zipped file

Some downloaded files end in `.zip` instead of `.exe`. When you double-click on the file, it will display an error message (or do nothing at all).

Zipped files are compressed. Several files (or one large file) are compressed into one smaller file for faster downloading. You will need to unzip the files before you can use them.

To unzip the files, you will need a program like WinZip. Download WinZip at `www.winzip.com`. It is free and will unzip most files you download from the Internet.

What Can Go Wrong?

Here are a few common problems people experience when trying to download files:

Downloading won't start

Problem: You click on a download link in a Web site, and nothing happens (or you get an error message).

Solution 1: The FTP server might be busy with too many other people attempting to download at the same time. Try again in a few minutes or later in the day.

Solution 2: Your browser may not be configured to automatically download the file. If clicking on the download link does not initiate a download, try this: in Internet Explorer, right click (click the rightmost mouse button) on the download link. From the menu that pops up, select "Save Target As ..." In Netscape Navigator, hold down the `SHIFT` key while you click on the download link.

Download starts, but doesn't finish.

Problem: The dialog box disappears before the download is 100% complete.

Solution: A number of things can cause this, from static on the telephone line, to losing your connection with the FTP server. Try the download again. If it still fails to complete, try again in a few minutes or later in the day.

The file won't run when you click on it.

Problem: When you double click on the file, you see an error message.

Solution 1: The file could be zipped. Use WinZip to unzip the file (see the *"Zipped Files"* section).

Solution 2: The file could be corrupt. Delete it, and download it again.

What next?

There are two files you should download first:

1) WinZip: `www.winzip.com`

2) Anti-virus software:

Norton Anti-virus: `www.symantec.com/nav`

Dr. Solomon: `www.drsolomon.com/download/findvirus.cfm`

McAfee Anti-Virus: `www.mcafee.com/download/eval.asp`

Next, take a look at these sites for thousands of programs to download:

Shareware.com: `www.shareware.com`

Zdnet's Software Library: `www.hotfiles.com`

Softseek: `www.softseek.com`

Creating Your Own Web Site

You don't have to be a big company to put up a Web site on the Internet. You can create your own, personal Web pages for any number of reasons. You can use a personal page to share news and personal information with other family members. You can publish your own art or poetry. You can voice an opinion, or help a cause. You can talk about your hobbies, or put up a shrine to your favorite star.

Creating a personal Web page does not require much technical knowledge. All you really need is something to say, and a little imagination.

Step 1: Find A Home

Your Web page needs a home. In other words, someone has to host your site by storing it on their server and giving the world access to it. If you already have an account with an ISP, ask them if they provide free Web page hosting (most do, at no additional charge). Call your ISP for details.

You can also try a community. This is a Web site that offers free home pages to anyone who wants to join. Membership is usually free, and most communities will give you free tools to design your page as well. Often, a community site will group pages together into common areas of interest. So if your site is devoted to fishing, it will be grouped with other sites about outdoor activities.

Because community sites will host your page at no charge, they will usually sell advertising space on your page. You won't have any control over what types of ads appear on your page, or where they appear. If this bothers you, you may prefer to ask your ISP to host your page. An ISP will not put advertising on your page. But you might find that having your ISP host the page is a bit more confusing when you are just getting started.

ON THE WEB

Some of the most popular Web communities:

Geocities: www.geocities.com

Talk City: www.talkcity.com

Tripod: www.tripod.com

Step 2: Create Your Web Page

Decide What You Want to Say

Take some time to figure out what your purpose for the site is. Will it be a newsletter about family events? A collection of photos from your last family reunion? Your own inspirational poems? An advice column? A tribute to someone who has inspired you? Use your imagination. Don't worry if people will be interested in what you have to say; the Web brings people from all over the world together, and the world is a really big place. No matter what you say, it will speak to someone.

Once you have chosen a topic, collect the information you will need. For example, if the page will be devoted to your goldfish, collect pictures of them. If you plan to publish your poetry, gather it together.

Get the Right Tools

Most people are surprised to learn that Web pages, no matter how artistic they look, are really just text files. Web pages are written in HTML (Hypertext Markup Language) which tells your browser where to put text, what color to paint the background, and where to put pictures. HTML is really easy to learn. But here's even better news: although HTML is easy to learn, you don't even have to learn it to create a Web page.

Community sites will provide you with simple tools that will help you create a Web page without any technical knowledge at all. But, if you want to get a bit more creative, or if you have chosen to have your ISP host the site, you will need your own tools. And like so many things on the Web, the tools you need are available for free.

When you are getting started, look for a WYSIWYG editing tool. WYSIWYG (pronounced whizzy-wig) stands for What You See Is What You Get. Remember, Web pages are written in HTML text; it is difficult to know what they will really look like until you view them in a browser. A WYSIWYG editor will let you see the page you are working on as a browser would see it. That helps you forget about writing HTML, and concentrate on being creative.

Some free Web editing tools to try:

Web Express
`www.mvd.com/webexpress`

This is an easy to use, completely WYSIWYG editor. Web Express can help you create a basic page quickly and easily. It also supports more advanced features like forms, image maps, and cascading style sheets.

Webford
`wkweb4.cableinet.co.uk/jwalsh/webford/webford.htm`

If you are interested in learning HTML, Webford is a good tool. It includes a wizard to assist you in creating a new page. Adding new features to your page is as easy as filling out a form. Webford even lets you add advanced features like JavaScripts easily.

Learning HTML

It is not necessary to learn HTML before you create a Web page. However, HTML is not difficult to learn. Once you know the basics of HTML, it will be easier for you do design the Web page you envision. Even if you decide to use a WYSIWYG editor, you will find that knowing the basics of HTML helps.

Writing a basic Web page in HTML

HTML is basically text that is surrounded by formatting tags. The tags are written in brackets. For example, the tag for bold text is <b>. The sentence, "This is my **very first** Web page," would be written like this:

```
This is my <b>very first</b> Web page.
```

The <b> switches on the bold formatting, and the </b> switches it off. In a browser, the words in between the bold tags would appear **in bold print**.

Below is the HTML source for a complete Web page:

```
<html>

<head><title>My First Web Page
</title></head>

<body>

Write anything you want to say here.

<p>
```

(The "p" tag above started a new paragraph. You can add as many paragraphs as you would like by repeating the "p" tag.)

```
</body>

</html>
```

Type the above example into any text editor, like **Notepad**. Save the file as a text-only file. Name it `index.htm`. Then, open the file in your Web browser. Voila! You have created a Web page.

To open a file in your browser:

Internet Explorer

Click **File⇨Open...** Click the Browse button. Find "index.htm", and click the "Open" button..

Netscape Navigator

Click on **File⇨Open Page...** Choose your file, and click the "Open" button.

Of course, this is a very basic example of a Web page. But once you get the hang of writing HTML, it becomes very easy to create a unique and effective page of your own.

Add a Link

If you plan to create more then one page, or if you want to link your page to other sites on the Web, you will need to learn how to add a hyperlink to your page.

Suppose you are creating an online family photo album. Your main page (usually named `index.htm`) might be a list of family events, like birthday parties and holidays. Each event on the list is a link to another page, which contains all the photos from that event. Let's assume you have already created a page with photos from the party, and named it `jason1998.htm`. To link "Jason's Birthday Party, 1998", to the page with the birthday party photos, you would type:

```
<a href="jason1998.htm">Jason's
Birthday Party, 1998</a>
```

In your browser, "Jason's Birthday Party, 1998" will appear underlined and in blue, like a regular hyperlink.

You can also link to pages that are not on your own site. For example, imagine Jason has his own site. You could link to his site (or any page on his site) like this:

```
<a href="http://www.jason.com/birth-
day.htm"> Jason's site</a>
```

Add an Image

Adding an image that you already have to your page is easy. Just use a tag:

```
<img src="cake.gif" alt="Birthday cake
with candles">
```

`Src` stands for source and is the name of the image file. The `alt` text will appear if your visitor cannot see graphics, or has the graphics turned off in his browser. It will also appear in Internet Explorer when your visitor points her mouse cursor at the image. Use the `alt` text to describe the photo.

Getting an image to add to your page is a little more complicated. You can get images from clip art or stock photography. There are many collections of art on the Web, and many are available for your use, free of charge. Read the site carefully to ensure that you can use the images without violating copyright laws.

You can also scan your own photographs. If you do not own a scanner, take your photos to a copy center. They can scan photos for you, and put them on a floppy disk, for a small charge. If you scan them yourself, save them as a `.jpg` file, at 72 DPI (dots per inch).

If you have some artistic talent, you can draw pictures yourself, using any graphics program on your computer. If you don't have a favorite graphics program, try Paint Shop Pro (`www.jasc.com/psp.html`). It is shareware, but it has many of the features of a much more expensive program. Save the image you create as a `.gif` file.

Adding images to your page can really make it stand out. But avoid putting huge images, or too many images, on your Web page. They will take too long to load in most people's browsers, and many people won't wait around to see them.

ON THE WEB

Sources of free images on the Web:

The Mining Company's Guide to Web Clip Art
webclipart.miningco.com

Internet Baglady
www.dumpsterdive.com

Resources for Icons, Images, and Graphics
www.aphids.com/susan/imres

The Free Site
www.thefreesite.com

Learning More

The more you learn about HTML, the more creative you can be with your Web pages. There are many sites on the Web that provide information about HTML:

ON THE WEB

The Easiest HTML Guide For Beginners
`tips-tricks.com/begin.html`

A Beginner's Guide to HTML
`www.ncsa.uiuc.edu/General/Internet/WWW`

The Mining Company's Guide to HTML
`html.miningco.com`

The Bare Bones Guide to HTML (reference)
`www.werbach.com/barebones/barebone.html`

While you are learning, it is often helpful to view the source of someone else's Web page. If you see a page that you like, take a look at the source to see how it was done. You can view the source of any Web page:

Internet Explorer

View⇨Source

Netscape Navigator

View⇨Page Source

Design Tips

Feel free to be creative when you design your page. That said, keeping a few guidelines in mind will help you create a page that your visitors will find appealing and easy to read.

- **Keep your background simple.** Avoid bright colors, busy background images, and black backgrounds. These make it difficult for other people to read what you have to say. Stick with white or light colored backgrounds.
- **Don't overuse graphics.** Too many images on one page can make the page very slow to load on most people's browsers.
- **Don't overuse animations.** You can add an animated image to your page as easily as adding a regular image. One or two animations will really jazz up a page. But if your entire page is jumping and spinning, it can be extremely distracting and often annoying.
- **Don't go font crazy.** A rule of thumb in design is to avoid using more than two fonts on a page. Also, you cannot assume your visitors will have the same fonts that you do. Try viewing your page on a friend's computer. You might be surprised when all of the fancy fonts you used are gone.

Step 3: Publish Your Site

Once you create your site, you will have to publish it. Generally, this means you will copy the pages (and images) from your computer to a web server. You will need an **FTP** program (File Transfer Protocol) to copy your files. If your ISP will be hosting the site, call and ask for the settings you will need to **upload** your site.

ON THE WEB

A few shareware FTP programs to try:

> ***WS_FTP:***
> www.ipswitch.com
> ***CuteFTP:***
> www.cuteftp.com
> ***Fetch (for the Mac):***
> www.dartmouth.edu/pages/softdev/fetch.html

Promoting Your Site

Once you spend all that time creating your page, you will want people to see it. Of course, you can announce it to all your friends via e-mail. But if you want to announce your new site to the world, you will have to do a little online promotion.

ON THE WEB

Try these free services that will list your sites with several search engines at once:

> ***Simple Submit:***
> www.verysimple.com/submit
> ***Submit It!:***
> www.broadcaster.co.uk

You can choose to join a Web Ring. A Web Ring is a collection of sites on a particular topic, linked together. Once you find one site in the ring, you can go forward or backward to another site. Or, you can jump randomly to a site. Web rings are free to join. To find a Web Ring for your topic, check www.webring.org.

You can also join a banner exchange. These free services allow you to advertise on other people's sites. In exchange, you provide space for other people to run ads on your site. The services are free, and are supported by some paid advertisers. Try the Link Exchange, at `www.linkexchange.com`.

Banner exchanges usually put your site in a category, so hopefully the ads that appear on your site will relate to your topic, and your ads will run on related sites as well. However, sometimes the categories are very general, and you don't have veto power over any particular ads. One father had the unpleasant experience of showing the page he had just created for his 8-year-old daughter to her - only to see an ad for an "adult entertainment' site.

PART III:

Staying Safe

In this section, you will discover how to:

- stay safe while shopping on the Internet
- protect your privacy while surfing
- avoid viruses
- keep your children safe
- create your own Web site

Staying Smart, Safe, and Secure

Safety, personal security, and privacy on the Internet are important issues. For the most part, using your common sense will help you steer clear of any sharks lurking in the surf. Read this section for tips on keeping yourself and your family safe.

Safe Shopping

Let's start with the question most people ask: Is it safe to shop on the Internet?

Assuming you are armed with information, and you are using common sense, the answer is yes. Here are some things you should know before you shop:

1. Always use your credit card

This is important for two reasons. First, when you use a credit card for an Internet purchase, you can dispute the charges if you have trouble with the company later.

Second, if someone is able to steal your credit card number, your liability is limited to $50. (Ask your credit card company for details.) Some Internet merchants, like Amazon.com (`www.amazon.com`) and Expedia (`expedia.msn.com`), even offer to pay that amount for you.

So, how likely is it that someone will steal your credit card number from the Internet? You might be surprised to hear that shopping at a reputable online store with a credit card is statistically safer than using your card in the real world.

Why safer? Think about how you use credit cards in the real world. In a restaurant, you hand your signed card to a waiter, who disappears with it for several minutes. When ordering from a catalog, you read it over the phone to a stranger. Fraud always involves another person, who has access to your credit card number.

When you shop online, your credit card number is sent from your computer to the store's computer. No other person sees the number. Often, the store's computer send the number along to the credit card company for processing, which means the store's computer does not even see the number.

Of course, people are concerned about the number being intercepted by a thief on the way to the store or the credit card company. For this reason, you want to be sure to shop at **secure sites**.

2. Shop at secure sites

As recently as a couple of years ago, there was no secure way of sending credit card information over the Internet. But **secure server** technology has made Internet commerce very safe. Secure servers protect your credit card numbers (and other private information) from being intercepted by a thief. In addition, they will **encrypt** (scramble) the information. So, even if someone was able to steal the information, he would not be able to read it.

To take advantage of the security this technology offers, you need to check two things: (1) that the store has a secure server and (2) uses a browser (such as Internet Explorer or Netscape Navigator) that supports secure transaction technology.

To determine if you are on a secure server when you are ready to give credit card information, check the bottom of your browser. (You can also take a look at the Web site address. If it starts with `https://`, it is a secure site - the "s" stands for secure.)

Internet Explorer

(and Netscape Communicator) Look for a closed padlock in the lower right corner of the browser.

Netscape Navigator

Look for an unbroken key in the lower left corner.

If the site does not offer a secure server, use your best judgment. Reports of credit card fraud resulting from purchases at Internet sites are fairly infrequent, even at sites which do not use secure servers.

3. Check the return policies

Read the return policy before you purchase anything. Print the policy in case you need it later. Sites disappear and change overnight, so it is always a good idea to have a record.

4. Know who you are dealing with

Most Internet companies are reputable. But the Web does make it very easy for fly-by-night companies to open their doors to the public. In the beginning, it is a good idea to start with companies you know and trust.

If you are not sure of a company's reputation, ask around. Jot down the physical address and phone number, in case you have trouble finding the site later. If there is no physical address, try to find a phone number (or at least an e-mail address) and see if you can speak to a real person. If it is difficult to contact the company, you will want to know that before you purchase, not after you have a problem.

Also, remember that there is a difference between a sale by a business, and a sale from a private person. Many people sell merchandise through e-mail, newsgroups, auctions, and classified ads. Just as in the real world, your legal rights may be different with a private seller than with a business.

If You Are Still Unsure

Most online merchants understand that people may be more comfortable sending credit card numbers over the phone, fax, or postal mail. Stores will often give you several options to pay for merchandise. Use the method you are most comfortable with. Online shopping cannot be surpassed in terms of convenience, variety, and price, and there is no reason to miss out.

Protect Your Privacy

Who's watching you surf? You may not realize it, but many Web sites collect personal information about you while you are online. Most Web sites collect information about where you are coming from, what browser you are using, and what pages you view. Some collect even more personal information. Most sites will not abuse this information. But, you should be aware that when you surf the net, you are not anonymous. Someone is watching.

ON THE WEB

For the truly paranoid:

The Anonymizer
www.anonymizer.com

Visit The Anonymizer before you visit any other sites, and it will create a false identity for you. This false identity fools every other Web site you visit from there, shielding you from invasions of your privacy.

Cookies

A cookie is a file that some Web sites use to "remember" information about you and your visit. Rather than keeping the information on their server, they store it on your hard drive with the help of the browser.

The next time you return to the site, the information stored in the cookie is used to personalize your experience or save you time. For example, the cookie might remember your user name and password, so that you can automatically log on to the site. It might remember what types of products you like. Maybe it will welcome you by name.

Many people enjoy the convenience that cookies offer. However, the potential for abuse makes some people nervous. If you are worried about cookies, consider this:

1) Only the site that created the cookie can read it later. No other sites can access that information.

2) Cookies cannot actively collect personal information that you do not volunteer, like your e-mail address or your real name. If you type information into a form at a Web site, that information might be saved in the cookie.

If you are still uncomfortable about cookies, you can ask the browser to warn you before accepting a cookie.

Internet Explorer

In **View⇨Internet Options**, click the "Advanced" tab. Under "Security," look for "Cookies." Click "Prompt before accepting cookies." Or, you can click "Disable all cookie use."

Netscape Navigator

In View⇨Internet Options, under "Advanced," look for "Cookies." Click "Warn me before accepting a cookie." You can also choose "Do not accept cookies." A third choice, "Accept only cookies that get sent back to the originating server," is available for medium security.

ON THE WEB

Shareware is available to help you guard your cookie jar:

Cookie Crusher:
www.thelimitsoft.com/cookie.html

Cookie Pal:
www.kburra.com

Forms

Many Web sites will ask you to fill out a form. Often, the form is required for a "free registration." Once you fill out the form, you usually gain access to members-only sections of the site, or to receive a newsletter, or even a special discount.

Whenever you fill out an online form, the site is collecting the information. That information could be shared with other organizations. Often at the end of the form, there will be a statement saying that you would like to receive news and special offers via e-mail. If this bothers you, uncheck the box before submitting the form.

To be safe using forms:

1) Read their privacy policy. Many sites voluntarily post a privacy statement on their site. This statement lets you know exactly what information they are collecting from you and whether they intend to share it with anyone else.

2) Don't give out personal information like a Social Security number, bank account number, or even your address and phone number unless you are comfortable with the business, and the information is necessary for the transaction.

For more about privacy issues, visit The Center for Democracy and Technology (`www.cdt.org/privacy`).

E-Mail

Sending an e-mail is like sending a postcard. The message is there for anyone to read. Everyone knows you do not put sensitive or personal information on a postcard. It is a good idea to view e-mail the same way.

However, there is a way to make e-mail more private. PGP (stands for Pretty Good Privacy) is free software that can encrypt your e-mail messages. Encrypting e-mail is similar to putting your postcard in a privacy-lined envelope.

Here is how it works. Imagine you are sending a message to a friend. You would use a "private key" to encrypt (scramble) your message. Once the message is encrypted, it looks like gibberish. You send the message to your friend, who has your "public key." She uses this second key to unscramble your message and read it.

When PGP was first released, it caused quite a bit of controversy. The government was uneasy, because they were concerned that people would use encryption to hide illegal activity. They wanted to be able to read anyone's messages. But now, PGP is freely available. You can download a free version at `www.pgpi.com`.

Viruses

Real Viruses

A virus is software that attempts to effect your computer without your permission. Viruses do not spontaneously generate; they are written by someone for a specific purpose.

Most are benign; they don't do any real damage to your computer. For example, a benign virus might display an annoying message on your screen

A few are malignant. These attempt to do serious damage to your computer. A malignant virus might try to erase the data on your hard drive, or change the way your programs behave.

Viruses are transmitted through software. A virus might attach itself to a program you download from the Internet. A diskette you borrow from a friend might be infected. Even a program you purchase from a store, from a reputable company, might have a virus.

Here are a few things you should know about viruses:

1. If your computer starts behaving strangely, don't assume you have a virus. Power surges, memory shortages, hardware conflicts, and accidental bugs in software can all make your computer behave erratically. (If your television picture starts to fade or jump, do you assume it has a virus?)

2. Don't download suspicious-sounding files from questionable sites. Use common sense.

3. Invest in antivirus software. Update it frequently, since new viruses are written all the time. Use your antivirus software regularly.

4. Make a backup copy of important files on a regular basis. If a virus destroys any of your data, you can restore it later.

Virus Hoaxes

If you have an e-mail account, chances are that you sometimes receive computer virus alerts. One common message, called "Win A Holiday," warns you of a dangerous new virus circulating the Internet. It says that if you receive an e-mail message entitled "Win A Holiday," you should not open the message. If you do, it warns, a virus will erase your entire hard drive.

You might be surprised to learn that most virus alerts are completely false. Although computer viruses do exist, there are a lot of misconceptions about how widespread the problem is and how dangerous they are. Virus alerts that are circulated through e-mail sound official and dangerous, and prey on people's fears. Because of this, they are circulated indefinitely, sometimes for years. In fact, more time and energy is spent fighting virus hoaxes then is spent monitoring real viruses.

How can you tell if a virus alert you receive is a hoax or a real warning? Here are some signs:

1. Take a good look at the message. The following false alert, warning about a virus in the Budweiser Frogs screen saver, contains plenty of capital letters and exclamation points. This is typical of virus hoaxes as well as Internet scams in general.

A sample virus hoax:

SUBJECT: DANGER!!! VIRUS ALERT!!! BUDWEISER FROGS

DANGER!!! VIRUS ALERT!!!

This is a new twist. Someone is sending out a very desirable screensaver - the Budweiser Frogs. But if you download it, you will lose everything!!! Your hard drive will drash!!!

DO NOT DOWNLOAD THIS UNDER ANY CIRCUMSTANCES!!!

IT JUST WENT INTO CIRCULATION THIS WEEK, AS FAR AS WE KNOW. BE CAREFUL!

BELOW IS WHAT THE SCREENSAVER OFFER WOULD LOOK LIKE: File: BUDWEISER.EXE

(24643 bytes)

DL Time (28800 bps): < 1 minute

PLEASE DISTRIBUTE THIS TO AS MANY PEOPLE AS POSSIBLE...THANKS!

2. Almost every virus hoax tells you to forward it to everyone you know. This is how the message remains in circulation. Usually it tries to impress upon you how dangerous the virus will be for everyone. It wants to convince you that you will be doing everyone a favor if you pass the message along (but don't be fooled).

3. Most hoaxes will warn you not to read an e-mail with a particular title. One alert warned people not to read any messages entitled "RETURNED OR UNABLE TO DELIVER." However, anytime an e-mail cannot get through to the recipient, it is returned to you with this subject. If you happen to mistype your friend's e-mail address, you will never know the message did not get delivered until you read the "returned" message.

4. Beware of technical-sounding language. The message is meant to sound impressive, but it really does not make any sense. Many virus warnings claim the impossible. They may claim you can get a virus just by reading an e-mail with a particular title, or by visiting a Web site. One false alert warns about a virus that can physically damage your monitor, hard drive, mouse, or keyboard. This is impossible.
5. The message will sound official, and appeal to some authority. Many warnings, hoping to add credibility to their claims, announce that they were originally issued by the FCC, or Microsoft, or America Online. However, these organizations do not send virus warnings.

To add to the problem, many people forward virus alerts without knowing they are false. Just remember, everyone from the salesperson in your local computer store to executives in major corporations have been fooled by these warnings. The message you receive might have been forwarded by someone you know and trust, but it is still probably a hoax.

EXPERT ADVICE

Since most virus alerts you receive via e-mail are hoaxes, don't forward them to anyone else. If you are worried that the warning might be true, check with an authoritative source.

- **The U.S. Department of Energy's Computer Incident Advisory Capability (the CIAC) maintains a Computer Virus Database, which lists both real viruses and hoaxes:** ciac.llnl.gov/ciac/CIACVirusDatabase.html
- **You can also learn more at the Computer Virus Myths Home Page:** kumite.com/myths.
- **Most anti-virus companies have a web page containing information about known viruses and virus hoaxes. Try these:**

Symantic's AntiVirus Research Center: www.symantec.com/avcenter

Dr. Solomon's Virus Central: www.drsolomon.com/vircen

Keeping Kids Safe

Should Kids Be On The Internet?

The potential dangers the Internet poses for children have generated plenty of attention in the media. Parents are naturally concerned that the Internet might not be a safe place for their children at all.

People from all walks of life are on the Internet. As it continues to grow, the mix of citizens in Cyberspace becomes more similar to the mix of citizens in any real-world community. Consequently, there will be people on the Internet you will want to keep away from your children.

Think about it. Would you leave your young child unattended on a public street or even a playground? Of course not. There are dangers in the playground, in the street, even in your own neighborhood. But you don't keep your child indoors to protect him from harm. There are too many wonderful experiences awaiting outside - the beauty of nature, the education and social interaction at school, the wonder of a museum.

Would you let your teenager stay out until all hours of the night, not knowing where or with whom? No, you want to monitor your teen's activities; you want to know his or her friends as best you can.

Keeping your kids away from the Internet is, in many ways, like locking them indoors, away from friends and experiences. Allowing kids to use the Internet, without guidance, is like letting them run free in the real world. As long as you are taking safety precautions, you can feel comfortable allowing your children to benefit from the best of what the Internet has to offer: a richness of experience, opportunities for learning, varied social interactions, and a comfort with technology which will be critical to their future.

The Internet vs. Television

Many parents wonder if they should limit children's time on the Internet, as they do with television. The difference between the Internet and television is important to understand: television is passive, while the Internet is active. The Internet has been referred to as a "self-directed learning experience." A child, by clicking hyperlinks and exploring further, actively seeks the information he is interested in. Compare it to a set of books. If your child wanted to spend hours in the library, choosing different books to learn more about any subject that interested him, would you object? The self-directed learning experience made possible on the Internet can be just as valuable.

Don't be concerned solely with the amount of time spent online. Instead, be concerned with the **quality** of their online time, and the **balance** of that time with other activities like physical exercise, family time, school responsibilities, and "face time" (real-world social interaction).

What Are The Risks?

There are primarily three types of risks that should concern you:

(1) Exposure to inappropriate material. It is possible (although not very common) for young children to stumble accidentally onto an inappropriate site; it is also possible (and more likely) for older children to intentionally seek out inappropriate material. To combat either possibility, consider using filtering software. Or, choose an ISP who will filter inappropriate sites for you.

(2) Improper contact with strangers. Certain areas of the Internet pose a higher risk than others: chat rooms, bulletin boards, newsgroups, and instant messages. The rules you set concerning these areas should depend on the age of your children .

ON THE WEB

Software that can help you or restrict or monitor children's online activities:

> ***NetNanny:***
> www.netnanny.com
>
> ***CyberSitter:***
> www.solidoak.com
>
> ***Cyber Patrol:***
> www.cyberpatrol.com
>
> ***Children's Internet Browser:***
> www.chibrow.com/informat.htm
>
> ***Cyber Snoop:***
> www.cyber-snoop.com

(3) Invasion of privacy. Obtrusive marketers are actually a much more prevalent threat to your family than offensive material or strangers. They will often ask children directly for personal information.

Do's and Don'ts For Parents

Do's:

- Set rules for online behavior. Print these rules, and post them right next to the computer. Discuss the rules with your children. Make sure they understand why following each rule is important.
- Set your Home button to go to a safe place. Let your children know they can always "go Home" if they ever find themselves in a place that makes them feel uncomfortable. (See the *"Getting the Most Out of Your Browser"* section.)
- Educate yourself. Spend time on the Internet. The more comfortable you are online, the better equipped you will be to protect your kids.

- Spend family time online. Keep the computer in a family room, not in one sibling's room. Whenever possible, go online as a family. Plan a vacation together. Pick out a movie. Let your kids show you their favorite sites.
- Supervise your children's time in Cyberspace as much as possible. Don't let them stay online unattended, for too long.

Don't:

- Don't keep kids off the Internet entirely. The benefits far outweigh the potential dangers. Being comfortable with technology is essential for the future of today's children. Understand and encourage your child's curiosity. Be careful, but be reasonable.
- Don't expect filtering software to do your job for you. Don't think you can let kids go unattended for long periods of time just because you set up software. Filtering software cannot protect children from every danger on the Internet. Plus, many older children can (and will) outsmart the software.
- Don't overreact if your kids come to you with a problem. If a child shows you an offensive site or a shocking message, your first response might be to take away Internet access, or blame the child. Instead, take a calmer approach. Remember, you want to encourage your children to be open with you, and bring problems to you.

Rules For Young Children

1. **I will not give out any personal information** before asking my parents' permission, like my
    - **real name,**
    - **home address,**
    - **phone number,**
    - **password,**

- **school name,**
- **parent's names, or**
- **credit card numbers.**

2. **I will not answer messages that are mean**, make me uncomfortable, threaten me, or use bad language.
    - **If I see anything that makes me uncomfortable, I will "go Home."**
    - **If I get a bad e-mail message, I will show the message to my parents immediately.**
3. **I will not agree to meet someone in real life** that I meet online. If anyone wants to meet me, I will tell my parents.
4. **I will remember that some of the things people say on the Internet are not true.** Some people are not who they say they are. Some adults might pretend to be kids.
5. **I will never send anyone a picture** of myself or my family without asking my parents' permission.

Rules For Older Children and Teens

Teens have to realize that the Internet is like a big city -- full of interesting places and people to meet, but with areas and people best avoided. Teens might need less supervision than young children, but they are actually more likely to get into trouble. Teens are more apt to seek out inappropriate sites. And teens are generally more secretive about what they are doing.

1. **I will protect my family's privacy.** I realize that whatever I post on the Internet is available for the entire world to see. I will avoid giving out personal information like my name, address, phone number, password, school name, parents' names, or credit card numbers in public places.
2. **If I decide to see in person anyone I've met online**, I will let my parents know first. I will arrange a meeting in a public place that I am familiar with. I will not go alone.

3. **I will not respond to any threatening,** suggestive, or obscene messages. I understand that responding just encourages the message writer.

4. **I will talk to my parents** about what I'm doing online. Although I want them to respect my privacy, I understand that talking to them will help them understand why I enjoy it. It will also help them to trust me.

5. **I will not harass other people,** threaten them, or be rude or disrespectful. I will respect other people's privacy.

EXPERT ADVICE

A Special Note to Teens

You already know what a great place the Internet is - you can keep in touch with friends, learn about anything, keep up with your favorite hobbies, sports, and music, and just have fun. Even if your parents are already on the Internet, you probably know a lot more then they do about what's out there.

This is your chance to teach your parents (and your teachers) something. They have a lot to learn about the Internet. And the more you can teach them, the more comfortable they will be with you spending lots of time online. Besides, they can probably teach you a few things about making good decisions and figuring out if what you read is true.

Think about it this way - if your parents figure out how much they can benefit from the Internet, they will understand why you really need that newer, faster upgrade!

Resources For Parents

1. Check out `www.safekids.com` and `www.safeteens.com`; both are great resources for parents and educators.

2. FBI safety tips, plus a place to report child pornography if you come across it:

   www.fbi.gov/kids/internet/internet.htm

3. "A Parent's Guide to the Internet," for parents, educators, law enforcement officials, and librarians:

   www.familyguidebook.com

4. Parents' Guide to Cyberspace, from the American Library Association: www.ala.org/parentspage

5. Many more resources are available online. Go to any search engine and type in the keywords kids Internet safety or children Internet safety.

PART IV:

Take a Guided Tour of the Web

In this section, take a guided tour of the best and most useful sites the Web has to offer. Sites are listed from Arts & Literature to Travel.

The Best & Most Useful Sites To Know

Here are ten sites (in ten categories) that are great sites to start your Web adventure. Listed are some of the most popular, most useful, and most informative sites on the entire World Wide Web.

Search Engine/Index

Yahoo

`www.yahoo.com`

News

CNN

`www.cnn.com`

Sports

ESPN SportsZone

`www.espn.com`

Weather

The Weather Channel

`www.weather.com/weather/us`

Travel

Expedia

`http://expedia.msn.com`

Business & Finance

The Wall Street Journal Online

`www.wsj.com`

Government

IRS Digital Daily

www.irs.treas.gov

Free Software

Hotfiles

www.hotfiles.com

Games

Happy Puppy

www.happypuppy.com

Education

The Kids Locker Room

www.peg.apc.org/~balson

CATEGORY: Arts & Literature
ACTIVITY: Buy theater tickets

Ticketmaster

www.ticketmaster.com

Yes, you can buy tickets online at Ticketmaster. But that's not even the best part of this site. Tickmaster's database of performances in major cities across the country doubles as a theatrical calendar. Find shows by city (including New Orleans) or venue. Visiting New York next Spring? Check out a listing of the shows on any date next year.

When you are ready to order tickets, check the seating charts and theater layouts. You can even print out directions to the theater. Order the tickets online using Ticketmaster's secure server or charge by phone. You can even buy merchandise and soundtracks from the top shows. Local venues include the Saenger, the Orpheum, and the Contemporary Arts Center.

Local Interest:

The Contemporary Arts Center
www.cacno.org

New Orleans Opera Association
www.neworleansopera.org

Gambit Weekly
www.bestofneworleans.com/frames/mataMain.html

Jefferson Performing Arts Society
www.jpas.com

Louisiana Philharmonic Orchestra
www.gnofn.org/nlpo

Also Worth a Look:

Gilbert & Sullivan Archive
diamond.idbsu.edu/gas/GaS.html

Phantom of the Opera Home Page
phantom.skywalk.com

CATEGORY: Arts & Literature
ACTIVITY: Visit a Museum

Paris WebMuseum

sunsite.unc.edu/wm/net

A visit to the Paris WebMuseum brings you about as up close and personal as you can get to art without travelling to Europe. This site is an art museum containing all of the classics and more. Take a guided tour of each piece by category (like gothic, renaissance, or Pop Art) or by artist (Rembrandt, Picasso, Monet, Leonardo). Want to take a closer look at Whistler's Mother? Just click to view a large, nicely detailed image.

The site is easy to navigate. And, since everything except the art itself is text-based, it loads very quickly. Find a painting you love? While viewing the large version, right click with your mouse and select "Set as Wallpaper."

Local Interest:

New Orleans Museum of Art
www.noma.org

Historic New Orleans Collection
www.hnoc.org

New Orleans Historic Voodoo Museum
www.voodoomuseum.com

Louisiana State Museum
www.crt.state.la.us/crt/museum/lsmnet3.htm

Also Worth a Look:

Metropolitan Museum of Art
www.metmuseum.org

National Museum of Natural History
www.mnh.si.edu

Guide to Museums and Cultural Resources on the Web
www.lam.mus.ca.us/webmuseums

National Civil Rights Museum
www.mecca.org/~crights

CATEGORY: Arts & Literature
ACTIVITY: Go to the Library

Library of Congress

www.loc.gov

The federal government has been on the Internet since the beginning, and they know how to do it in style. The Library of Congress offers a fascinating site that is definitely worth a visit.

Sections include American Memory, a multimedia library, which tells American history through photos, sounds, and video. For more current events, visit THOMAS to read the full text of bills under consideration by Congress. Past exhibits are always on display here, so you can view "The Gettysburg Address" and "The Scrolls of the Dead Sea" without making the trek to Washington. Plus, you will find a full range of research tools and library services for teachers and librarians.

Local Interest:

New Orleans Public Library
www.gnofn.org/~nopl

Tulane University's Special Collections
www.tulane.edu/~lmiller/SpecCollHomePage.html

Also Worth a Look:

The New York Public Library
www.nypl.org

Category: Career & Money
Activity: Find a Job

America's Job Bank

www.ajb.dni.us

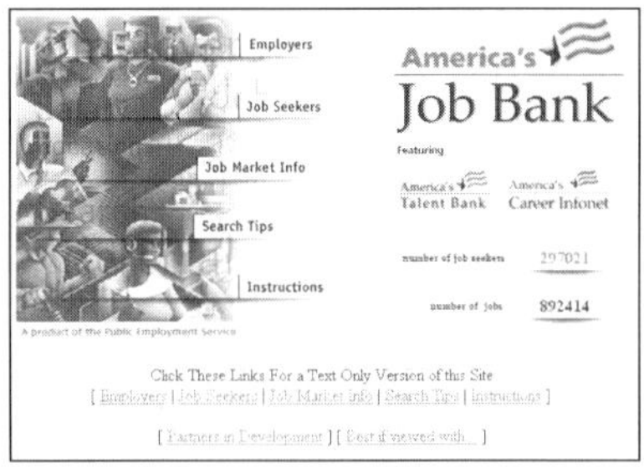

America's Job Bank lists over 600,000 jobs across the country (including a long list of jobs in Louisiana), making it one of the largest source for job postings on the Internet. At a recent visit, available jobs outnumbered applicants by three to one - great odds for job seekers. These are not just technical jobs either; categories include "Construction" and "Media and the Arts."

The sites listed below offer free resources, like advice on writing resumes and cover letters, salary comparisons, and information about employers. Since the Internet is open 24 hours a day, seven days a week, you can access these resources anytime, regardless of your schedule.

Local Interest:

NOLA Live with the Times-Picayune (searchable classified ads)
www.nola.com

Gambit Weekly Classifieds
www.bestofneworleans.com/frames/capMain.html

Medical Jobs in Louisiana
www.medjoblouisiana.com

Louisiana Civil Service
www.dscs.state.la.us

Also Worth a Look:

What Color Is Your Parachute: Job Hunting Online
www.washingtonpost.com/parachute

CareerMosaic
www.careermosaic.com

Monster Board
www.monsterboard.com

The Riley Guide
www.dbm.com/jobguide

Category: Career & Money
Activity: Get Stock Quotes

The Motley Fool

www.fool.com

The Motley Fool's goal is to "inform, educate and amuse the individual investor." At the site, you can learn about the Fool's approach to investing by attending "Fool's School." There you can study the 13 steps to investing Foolishly, and learn how to value stocks. You can read one of their informative daily columns. Or visit the forum, where you can discuss specific stocks or industry trends with other forum members around the world.

The Motley Fool's philosophy says that an individual can learn to successfully manage and invest money. The key to investment success, they say, is to do your homework. This site's refreshing approach might be just the thing to start you on the road to riches.

Also Worth a Look:

The Wall Street Journal
www.wsj.org

Microsoft Investor
investor.msn.com

Invest-O-Rama
www.investorama.com

E*Trade (online discount brokerage)
www.etrade.com

Real Time Quotes
rtq.thomsoninvest.net

JustQuotes
www.justquotes.com

CATEGORY: Computers & Technology
ACTIVITY: Buy a Computer

Cyberian Outpost

www.cybout.com

Why drive around town to find the best deals on computers and accessories? Try Cyberian Outpost. This site has full descriptions of products, plus editorial reviews designed to help you make a better decision. Cyberian Outpost claims to carry only those products meeting their quality standards. Browse PCs or Macs, search for a brand name, or check out the bargain basement for dozens of markdowns. Cyberian Outpost carries software and accessories as well.

Unlike a paper catalog, the online catalog is updated in real-time, so the latest products and prices are listed. You can order over the Web or over the phone.

Customize a Computer System:

Gateway 2000
www.gw2k.com

Dell Computer Company
www.dell.com

Computer Discount Warehouse
www.cdw.com

Online Auctions and Lowest-Price Searches:

Internet Shopping Network
www.isn.com

E*Market Live
www.emarketlive.com

Price Watch
www.pricewatch.com

CATEGORY: Computers & Technology
ACTIVITY: Get free software

ZDNet's Software Library

www.hotfiles.com

Ready to outfit your computer with some new bells and whistles? ZDNet's software library has over 10,000 programs available, including freeware, shareware, and demo software. Each has a review and a rating to help you determine if it is worth the time to download.

Check the front page for new and hot files, or do a search for exactly the type of program you need. Categories include screen savers, games, utilities, small business, and graphics. Your best bet? Try the top 10 downloads lists and see what all the fuss is about.

Also Worth a Look:

C|Net's Software.com
www.software.com

Filez
www.filez.com

Virtual Software Library
www.shareware.com

The Shareware Shop
www.bsoftware.com

The Mining Company's Guide to Shareware
shareware.miningco.com

Palm Pilot Software
www.zdnet.com/swlib/pilotsoftware

Category: Entertainment
Activity: Catch The Latest Hollywood News and Gossip

Mr. Showbiz

www.mrshowbiz.com

Mr. Showbiz is called "an entertainment magazine with moving parts." It's certainly fun to play with. Updated daily, Mr. Showbiz shares his fresh and entertaining views on the stars we love and everything they are up to.

Give him your opinion on celebrity nudity in the "Water Cooler Poll," let him help you decide "To TV or Not To TV," or read up on your favorite recording artists in the "Wall of Sound." Besides new daily headlines and movie reviews, there are profiles on over 600 celebrities. Actually, you never quite know what you will find next at Mr. Showbiz; you only know it will be fun.

Also Worth a Look:

E! Online
www.eonline.com

Hollywood Online
www.hollywood.com

Starbuzz
www.starbuzz.com

CATEGORY: Entertainment
ACTIVITY: Get Movie Times & Tickets

Yahoo! Movies

movies.yahoo.com

Yahoo! Movies is a one-stop shop for movie listings. Type in a movie name (or choose from the top ten at the box office) and your zip code. Yahoo! serves up showtimes, matinee times, and movie listings for the entire week at several area theaters. Click on a theater, and you can see all the movie listings for the week, plus an address and phone number. Yahoo! will even draw you a map to the theater.

Every movie links to a page with running times and links to information about the stars, reviews, and even movie trailers. Loved the latest adventure flick? Yahoo! will suggest "Matches" - other movies on video that you might also enjoy.

Local Interest:

The Palace Theatre
www.thepalacetheatre.com

New Orleans Film & Video Festival
www.neworleansfilmfest.com

New Orleans Video Access Center
www.gnofn.org/~novac

Also Worth a Look:

The Internet Movie Database
www.imdb.com

Mr. Cranky RatesThe Movies
www.mrcranky.com

Film.com
www.film.com

Ain't It Cool News
www.aint-it-cool-news.com

Hype!
www.hype.com

CATEGORY: Entertainment
ACTIVITY: Rent a Video

Reel

www.reel.com

Reel calls itself "The Planet's Biggest Video Store," and yes, they actually rent movies online. Over 35,000 titles are available, with a 7-day rental costing about $4.50. They ship the movies to your home, along with a postage-paid mailer you can use for an easy return.

Reel has movies for sale, also. They feature over 80,000 titles, on VHS, Laser Disk, and DVD formats. For a real bargain, head to the used movies section. You will find thousands of previously viewed VHS tapes, cheap. Every week they feature 50 movies available for under $5. And if you are a real movie buff, you will want to stop by their rare movies section. You can rent, buy, and sell hard to find movies, including out of print titles.

Looking for a movie you haven't already seen a hundred times? Reel uses artificial intelligence to recommend movies you might like, based on your favorites. And for another great movie idea, they recommend a Pick of the Day. This is a movie you may not have caught at the box office. A quick look at the Movie Matches to see if you liked any similar films will predict if this one is worth a try.

Also Worth a Look:

NetFlix (DVD rentals and sales)
www.netflix.com

Home Film Festival
www.homefilmfestival.com

Best Video (classic, foreign, cult, and hard-to-find movies)
www.bestvideo.com

Laser Discovery Online (laser disk and DVD rentals and sales)
www.laserdiscovery.com

Video Vault (cult movies)
www.laserdiscovery.com

Category: Entertainment
Activity: Follow a Band

Worldwide Internet Live Music Archives

www.wilma.com

WILMA, short for Worldwide Internet Live Music Archives, is the place to visit for live concerts, tour dates, and club listings for the entire U.S. You can search the database by artist, type of music, or venue. WILMA covers shows in festivals and tiny nightclubs all over the country, in musical genres as diverse as Country, Jazz/Blues, Rock, and New Age.

Sign up for WILMA's free notification service, and you will receive e-mail alerts when your favorite artists are heading to town. You can also learn more about the music by listening to streaming audio clips, watching video clips, and reading profiles of the artists.

Local Interest:

- ***Cowboy Mouth***
  `www.cowboymouth.com`
- ***The Neville Brothers***
  `www.nevilles.com`
- ***Tipitina's Schedule***
  `offbeat.com/tipitinas`
- ***House of Blues***
  `www.hob.com`
- ***Louisiana Music Archive and Artists Directory***
  `www.satchmo.com/nolavl`
- ***The Iguanas***
  `www.iguanas.com`

CATEGORY: Entertainment
ACTIVITY: Listen to the Radio

Radio Free New Orleans

neworleansonline.com/rfno.htm

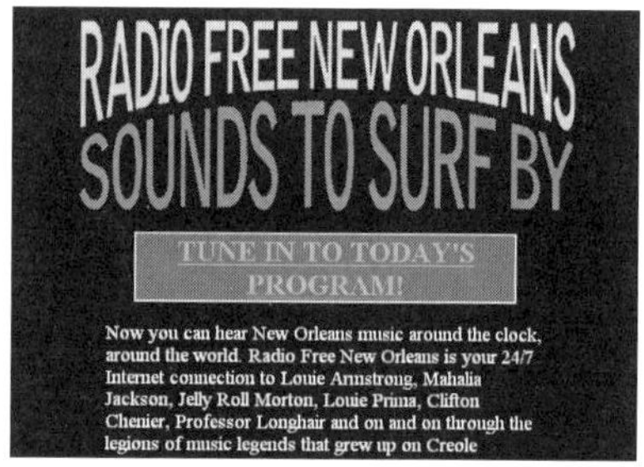

The New Orleans Tourism Marketing Corporation has set up Radio Free New Orleans. Similar to a virtual jukebox, Radio Free New Orleans plays recordings of jazz, blues, and gospel, all day long.

To listen to RFNO's streaming audiocast, download the RealPlayer plug-in at `www.real.com`. Then sit back and enjoy. Every day is a new style of music, from Monday's traditional jazz to Friday's Funk-day to Gospel on Sunday. Listen long enough and you will hear stories about New Orleans culture and music in between the clips. If you are stuck in an office building all day, either in the CBD or far from home, this might be just the thing you need to keep your toes tapping.

Local Interest:

WWOZ (live netcast)
`www.wwoz.org`

Also Worth a Look:

Real Player
`www.real.com`

National Public Radio
`www.npr.org`

Car Talk
`cartalk.com`

AudioNet
`www.audionet.com`

net.radio
`www.netradio.net`

TalkAmerica (live talk programming 24 hours a day)
`www.talkamerica.com`

Old Time Radio (vintage radio shows)
`www.old-time.com`

Category: Food
Activity: Get a Recipe

Arnaud's

www.arnauds.com/recipes.html

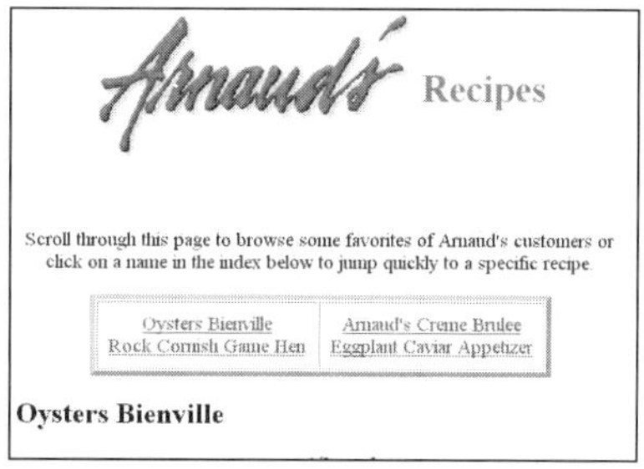

Here's a great trend on the Web that every food lover hopes will catch on: famous restaurants posting their customers' favorite recipes on the Internet. Just try to read these descriptions without your mouth watering. Better yet, print a few and try them out.

Besides the great New Orleans recipes, you can find recipes from every culture on the Web. From low fat to completely indulgent, check out a few of the links below before your next trip to the grocery.

Local Interest:

Best of New Orleans - Recipes
`www.bestofneworleans.com/frames/cuisMain.html`

Southern Yat Hysterical Society
`www.southernyatclub.com/recipes.html`

In the Kitchen with Frank Davis
`ww2.wwl-tv.com/franks_kitchen/franks_kitchen.htm`

Chef Paul Prudhomme
`www.chefpaul.com/recipes.html`

Also Worth a Look:

I Need My Chocolate
`www.qrc.com/~sholubek/choco/start.htm`

Epicurious Food
`food.epicurious.com`

The Mining Company's Guide to Low Fat Cooking
`lowfatcooking.miningco.com`

Mimi's Cyber Kitchen
`www.cyber-kitchen.com`

Recipe Archive Index
`www.vuw.ac.nz/cgi-bin/recipes`

CATEGORY: Food
ACTIVITY: Choose a Restaurant

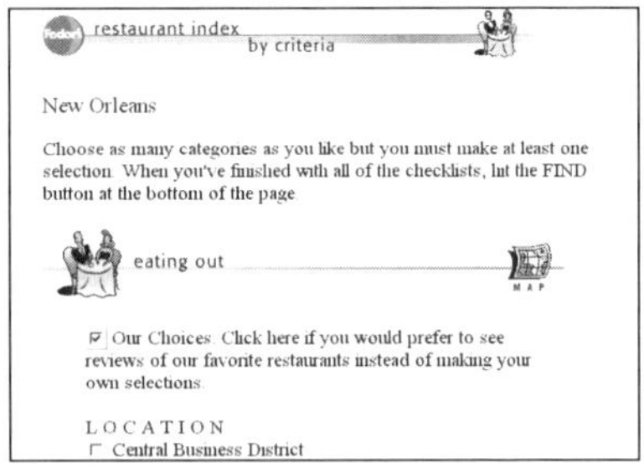

Fodor's Restaurant Guide

www.fodors.com

If you are always ready to try a new restaurant, but can't think of one at the right time, try Fodor's Restaurant Guide. Fodor's has a database of restaurants in all price ranges and cuisine. Ask the Guide to recommend a restaurant based on past reviews.

Or, pick an area (from the Ninth Ward to Metairie), a cuisine (Creole, Italian, Steak Houses...) and a price range. Fodor's will supply you with a list of restaurants that meet your criteria, along with all the information you need: an overview of the menu, sample courses, address, phone number, days open, reservations required, dress code, and credit cards accepted.

If you are travelling, use Fodor's to generate a list of "don't miss" restaurants near your hotel. All major cities are covered. Bon appetit!

Local Interest:

New Orleans Restaurant Directory (order online for pickup or delivery)
food.from.net/near/New+Orleans,+LA

New Orleans Online Dining Guide
neworleansonline.com/guide-rest.htm

The New Orleans Virtual Dining Guide
www.yatcom.com/neworl/dining/resttop.html

Foodfest
www.neworleans.com/foodfest

Also Worth a Look:

Excite Restaurant Review Finder
city.net/forms/restaurants

Menus Online
www.menusonline.com

Fast Food Finder (nutritional information on fast food)
www.olen.com/food

Category: Food
Activity: Order Gourmet Food

Virtual Vineyards

www.virtualvin.com

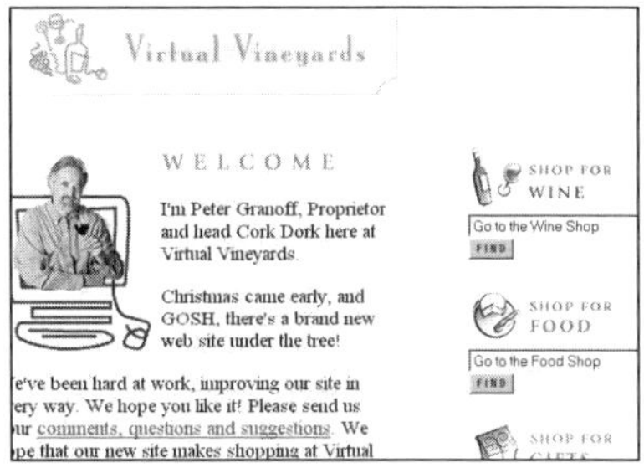

Wine connoisseurs have flocked to this site since its opening in 1994. An intelligent, informative site, Virtual Vineyards is as much a wine club as a shop. Serious wine buffs are advised on wines produced by small, well-respected wineries. For wine novices, Virtual Vineyards provides a unique learning experience, with interactive "tasting charts" and columns like "Ask the Cork Dork."

Sign up for the sampler program and have several recommended bottles arrive at your doorstep each month. Virtual Vineyards also sells gourmet food, in case all of this drinking makes you hungry.

Local Interest:

New Orleans Over Night
www.nuawlins.com

Cajun Spice Company
www.cajunspiceco.com

Haydel's Bakery
www.haydelbakery.com

Orleans Coffee Exchange
www.orleanscoffee.com

Also Worth a Look:

Godiva Chocolatier
www.godiva.com

Le Village
www.levillage.com

NetGrocer
www.netgrocer.com

The Gourmet Food Store
www.gourmetstore.com

CATEGORY: Freebies
ACTIVITY: Enter Online Sweepstakes and Contests

Sweepstakes Online

www.sweepstakesonline.com

Ever wonder if anybody really wins all of those cars, vacations, stereos, and cash given away in contests every week? Well, many people consider winning contests to be a hobby. Sites like Sweepstakes Online make it easier, with listings of hundreds of giveaways such as Cadillacs, trips to Vegas, and tickets to the World Series. Save your stamps and enter dozens of sweepstakes online.

Did you know there is a difference between sweepstakes and contests? Sweepstakes require no special skill and can be entered daily, weekly, or monthly. Contests test you in trivia, writing, photography, or recipes. You can also choose what to enter by the prize - would you rather win a boat, a bike, or a computer? Sweepstakes Online will even help you stack the odds in your favor with tips and tricks from the "pros". Good luck!

Also Worth a Look:

ContestWorld
www.contestworld.com

Get Rich Click
www.getrichclick.com

The Big Sweepstakes Page
www.ntplx.net/~nparker

The Mining Company's Guide to Contests and Sweepstakes
contests.miningco.com

Win On The Net
www.winonthe.net

CATEGORY: Freebies
ACTIVITY: Clip Coupons

Internet Coupon Directory

www.directcoupons.com

While you are surfing, why not take the time to clip a few coupons? Spend just a few minutes, and you can collect enough coupons to pay the fifteen or twenty dollars you spend on Internet access every month.

You can find sites offering coupons for everything from baby formula to vacations. The Internet Coupon Directory lists coupon sites for national and regional grocery chains, national and local retail stores, Internet-only coupons, and Internet freebies. They also offer a free weekly newsletter, so you can keep up-to-date on savings.

Local Interest:

The Coupon Directory
`www.coupondirectory.com`

Also Worth a Look:

Piggy Bank Savers (Baby Supplies)
`www.sdx-tech.com/baby/costcut.htm`

Cool Savings
`www.coolsavings.com`

Coupons, Discounts, and Freebies
`free-n-cool.com`

Weekly Refunder
`www.wr2000.com`

Custom Coupon
`customcoupon.com`

CATEGORY: Fun & Games
ACTIVITY: Video & Computer Games

Happy Puppy

www.happypuppy.com

So many games, so little time - and money. Happy Puppy helps by listing over a thousand shareware, freeware, and demos of games available over the Internet. View screen shots and read reviews of the hottest games in categories like Action, Arcade, Sports, Flight Sims, and Board Games.

You will also find cheats, hints, news, and upgrades to games for both the PC and the Mac. Even better - plug in to cheats and walkthroughs for the latest console games on the Sega Saturn, Nintendo 64, and Sony Playstation. Still not enough? Happy Puppy has links to the latest Web-based games (Java and Shockwave) as well.

Also Worth a Look:

Professional Gamers League (go pro!)
`www.pgl.net`

Gamesmania
`www.gamesmania.com`

The Games Domain
`www.gamesdomain.co.uk`

UGO Network
`www.ugo.net`

Dwango (multiplayer network)
`www.dwango.com`

Category: Fun & Games
Activity: Contests and Game Shows

You Don't Know Jack

www.bezerk.com

Combine a wisecracking game show host, an offbeat sense of humor, and challenging trivia, and you've got You Don't Know Jack: The Netshow. The online version of the award-winning CD-ROM trivia game is just as fun and - better yet - completely free.

There are two new "episodes" posted to the Web each week, and there is a sports version as well. Unlike a TV game show, you can play anytime, day or night. But you will have to sit through a few commercials. Now that sounds like the real thing.

Also Worth a Look:

The Riddler
www.riddler.com

Yoyodyne
www.yoyo.com

Gamesville
www.gamesville.com

Wheel of Fortune
www.wheeloffortune.com

Jeopardy
www.jeopardy.com

CATEGORY: Fun & Games
ACTIVITY: Humor

Centre for the Easily Amused

www.amused.com

Want to waste some time? Don't miss the Centre for the Easily Amused. The Centre combs the Web for useless, funny, and sometimes completely ridiculous Web sites. All sites are listed under informative categories like "Sites That Do Stuff" and "Random Silliness." Don't have that much time to waste? Try the "Short Attention Span Site of the Week."

Where else can you find links to such classic sites as "Ask Carl the Magic Gnome," and "Roscoe the Cat's Amazing Live Litterpan Cam"? As if that weren't enough, the Centre has been busy adding its own random silliness to the Web: try "The Book of Eleven," billed as "An Online Collection of Brain Lint." If that's too intellectual for you, unwind in the "Amused Arcade" with a game of Peanut Butter and Jelly Wars ("The ultimate battle for supremacy on sandwich bread.").

Also Worth a Look:

Dancing Baby
www3.cd-music.com/~bobh/dancing-baby

Ha! (joke database)
www.hardyharhar.com

PythOnline (Monty Python)
www.pythonline.com

The Capt. James T. Kirk Sing-a-long Page
www.loskene.com/singalong/kirk.html

Alien Abduction Insurance Policy
www.ufo2001.com

GhostWatcher
www.flyvision.org/sitelite/Houston/GhostWatcher

CATEGORY: Fun & Games
ACTIVITY: Comic Strips

The Comic Zone

www.unitedmedia.com

United Media is home to the Peanuts gang and Dilbert, along with a number of other popular favorites. A handy drop-down box lets you jump to the latest episodes of "Rose is Rose," "Alley Oop," "Drabble," "For Better or For Worse," and a number of others. Check out the past few weeks of strips, grab icons and screen shots, and e-mail the author to let him know what you'd like to see next.

The Comic Zone is the home of the Dilbert Store and the Snoopy Shop, for ordering merchandise like toys, art, and clothing. If you have a really fast computer (a 300 megahertz Pentium II or faster) head for the Comic Explorer, a totally new way of looking at comic strips.

Also Worth a Look:

Universal Press Syndicate (Cathy, Garfield, and others)
`http://www2.uclick.com`

Doonesbury Town Hall
`www.doonesbury.com`

Dr. Katz: The Comic Strip
`www.comedycentral.com/katz/home/code/hm.strip.html`

Calvin and Hobbes Comics Gallery
`www.okidoki.nl/calvin_and_hobbes`

The Comics I Don't Understand page
`www.concentric.net/~Bbickel/cidu.shtml`

The Comics Hotlist (create your own personalized comics page)
`www.uta.fi/yhteydet/personalhl.html`

CATEGORY: Government
ACTIVITY: Pay Your Taxes

IRS Digital Daily

www.irs.treas.gov

It might be hard to believe, but the IRS Web site is actually... whimsical. You will see a whole new side to the IRS at this site. You can also get a head start on your tax returns.

The site is a self-service tax center, where you can download every tax form and instruction booklet, apply for an extension, even file your return automatically. The IRS keeps a handy countdown to April 15, making it easy for you to keep tabs on how many days you have left before the big deadline. Try the section that explains the tax regulations in "plain English," or, at least, as close as they can.

Also Worth a Look:

Turbo Tax Online
www.intuit.com/turbotax

SecureTax
www.securetax.com

Ernst & Young
www.ey.com/tax

Category: Government
Activity: Forward Your Mail/Relocate

U.S. Postal Service

www.usps.gov

How would you like to have a neighborhood post office with no crowds, no lines, with service 24 hours a day, seven days a week? That's what the Postal Service site claims. They offer most of the services you would find at a bricks-and-mortar post office: look up a zip code for any address, track your express mail package, order shipping supplies, apply for a passport, check postage rates, calculate shipping charges, even buy stamps.

You will also find a wealth of information on avoiding fraud, schedules of auctions of unclaimed items, and even the Wanted posters. If you are planning a move, visit MoversNet to change your address and register to vote in your new community.

Online Postal Services:

MoversNet
`www.usps.gov/store`

Shipping Supplies
`supplies.usps.gov`

Stamps Online
`www.usps.gov/fr_stamps.html`

U.S. Postal Service Virtual Store
`www.usps.gov/store`

Unforgettable Letters
`www.usps.gov/letters`

Also Worth a Look:

Fedstats (data from all different federal agencies)
`www.fedstats.gov`

The Great American Web Site (guide to government sites)
`www.uncle-sam.com`

Social Security Administration (Top 10 most requested services)
`www.ssa.gov/top10.html`

CATEGORY: Government
ACTIVITY: Keep an Eye on Washington

THOMAS

thomas.loc.gov

Internet has played a bigger part recently in keeping people informed about events in Washington. THOMAS is run by the Library of Congress, and was named after Thomas Jefferson. The entire Congressional Record of the United States, every bill put before Congress, and every committee report is on this site. You can research a bill, follow what your representative is doing, and get daily updates on current legislation.

Don't know the number of a bill? Go to "Congress in the News," where you can look up bills by the topics that recent news stories have covered. There is an alphabetical listing of every topic from Abortion to the Year 2000 Computer Problem and links every bill that relates to that topic.

Also Worth a Look:

The White House
www.whitehouse.gov

White House For Kids
www.whitehouse.gov/WH/kids/html/kidshome.html

Locate Your Lawmakers
www.pbs.org/point/pie/yourcongress

Congress.org
congress.org

U.S. Senate
www.senate.gov

U.S. House of Representatives
www.house.gov

The House Budget Committee
www.house.gov/budget

Office of the Majority Whip
majoritywhip.house.gov

Freedom Works: The Office of the House Majority Leader
freedom.gov

Category: Home & Garden
Activity: Buy a House

Realtor.com

www.realtor.com

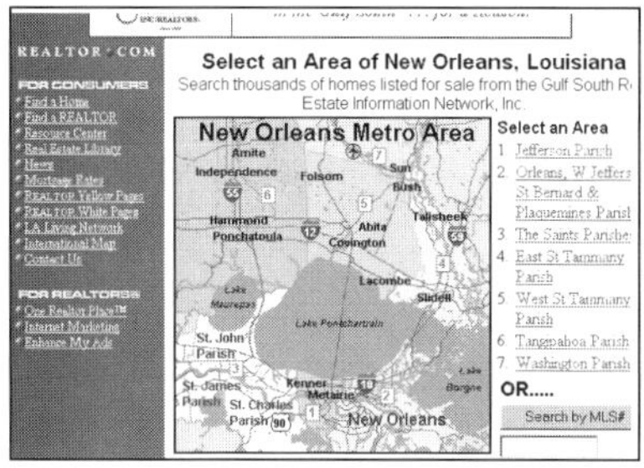

Now, this is convenient. Take a look at houses, townhouses, and condos available for sale in the metro New Orleans area (or just about any other area in the country) without going outdoors. The site is sponsored by the National Association of Realtors.

First, choose the parishes and the neighborhoods you are considering. Then, tell Realtor.com what you are looking for. Your search criteria can be very general, specifying a price range and minimum size. If you prefer, you can specify details like an older home, a corner lot, or a swimming pool. Then, go shopping. Houses are shown with full-color photos, room dimensions, price, and a link to the realtor's Web site. You can even print a map of the area and access community information, like school districts, crime reports, and environmental reports.

Local Interest:

Hibernia National Bank
www.hiberniabank.com

Louisiana International Mortgage Corporation
www.louisianamortgage.com

CountryWide
www.countrywide.com

Home By Net (sponsored by Bank One)
www.homebynet.com

Also Worth a Look:

Bank Rate Monitor (up-to-the-minute mortgage rates from local lenders)
www.bankrate.com

HomePath (sponsored by Fannie Mae)
www.homepath.com

Quicken Mortgage
mortgage.quicken.com

CATEGORY: Home & Garden
ACTIVITY: Do It Yourself

HouseNet

www.housenet.com

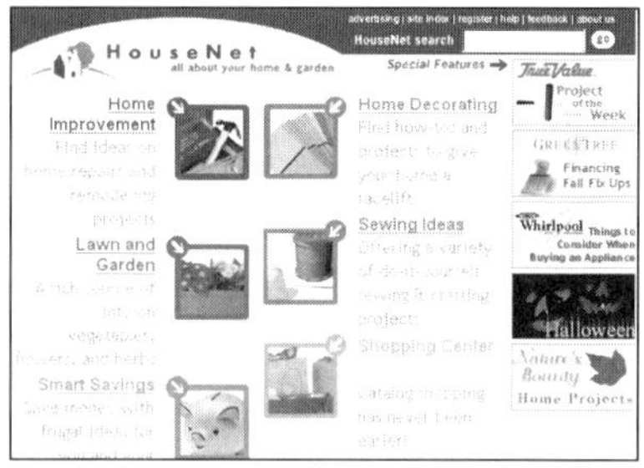

If you are thinking of tackling a home improvement project, your computer could be the most useful tool you own. Whether your project is as simple as installing a new doorbell or as complex as building a whole new kitchen, you will find a wealth of resources to help you get started, plan a budget, and do a professional-looking job.

HouseNet is run by husband and wife team Gene and Katie Hamilton. The Hamiltons have been chatting about home improvement online since 1991, and they have plenty of know-how to share. In addition to how-to articles, they offer a calculator you can use to figure out how much paint you will need to buy for any room.

And don't miss the "Cost of a Job" section, where they will help you determine if the improvements you have in mind are good do-it-yourself projects or if it would be cheaper to hire a professional.

Also Worth a Look:

Better Homes & Gardens Home Improvement Encyclopedia
www.bhglive.com/homeimp

Home Ideas
www.homeideas.com

Microsoft Home Advisor
homeadvisor.msn.com

This Old House
www.pathfinder.com/TOH

Home & Garden Television
www.hgtv.com

CATEGORY: Home & Garden
ACTIVITY: Plant a Garden

Gardening.com

www.gardening.com

If you have gardening questions, bring them here. The Plant Encyclopedia lists over 1,500 varieties, with illustrations, care instructions, and pest control advice. The Ortho Problem Solver diagnoses hundreds of problems for you. The Garden Site Directory points you to gardening resources all over the Internet, with reviews.

If you still have questions, try posing them in the forum, where members gather to discuss greenery matters. This site also features a Yellow Pages of garden centers, landscapers, and greenhouses. The Magazine Rack features reviews of electronic publications on the Internet.

Local Interest:

City Park Botanial Gardens Tour
`www.neworleans.com/citypark/facility.html#tours`

Also Worth a Look:

The Armchair Gardner
`armchairgardener.com`

Garden Web
`www.gardenweb.com`

Garden Escape
`garden.com`

The Virtual Gardener
`www.gardenmag.com`

HGTV's Gardendale
`www.hgtv.com/village/villages/gardendale/g.over.html`

Sherry's Greenhouse
`www.sherrysgreenhouse.com`

CATEGORY: Kid-Friendly Sites
ACTIVITY: Great Kids Sites

Nickelodeon

www.nick.com

Nickelodeon is a favorite site among the younger set, and it's no wonder. Official game reviewers Daggett and Norbert recommend crazy new games like "Disgruntled Warthog" and "Harriet the Spy's Spy Test" that kids can download.

Favorite TV shows like "AHHH! Real Monsters" and "Rugrats" are all here as well. Kids can meet other kids, find out about new hobbies, and really have some fun at this imaginative site.

Also Worth a Look:

Disney
www.disney.com

Sports Illustrated for Kids
www.sikids.com

Enchanted Forest at GeoCities
www.geocities.com/EnchantedForest

Worm World
www.nj.com/yucky/worm

A Girl's World
www.agirlsworld.com

Kids' Space
www.kids-space.org

PBS Online
www.pbs.org

Seussville
www.randomhouse.com/seussville

Coloring.com
coloring.com

CATEGORY: Kid-Friendly Sites
ACTIVITY: Finding Kid-Friendly Sites

Disney Internet Guide

www.dig.com

The Internet can be a scary place for young children. But there are some sites that can help steer them toward kid-friendly content and away from inappropriate material. Sites like Dig identify safe areas on the Web, so kids can be free to explore and interact.

Dig, short for Disney Internet Guide, is a search engine built specifically for kids. Every site listed in Dig has been hand-picked and reviewed by Disney staff members, ensuring that it is appropriate for families. Sites are listed in categories like "Animals & the Outdoors," "Learning & Life," and "Stories & Comics." Disney will also take you on an interactive tour of the Web. Tours depart from Dig every Tuesday at 5:00 p.m. and last about an hour. If you ever miss a tour, you can catch up in the archives. Each tour has a theme; recent tours have covered dinosaurs, great museums, and space.

Also Worth a Look:

Yahooligans
www.yahooligans.com

American Library Association
www.ala.org/parents

Infoseek Kids' Directory
http://www.infoseek.com/Topic/Kids_and_Family

CATEGORY: Kid-Friendly Sites
ACTIVITY: Finding Help With Homework

Ask Jeeves For Kids

www.ajkids.com

If your kids ever ask you one of those questions you just don't have a quick answer to, send them to Jeeves.

At the Ask Jeeves for Kids site, kids can ask important questions like "Why is the Mona Lisa smiling?" and "Who is the king of Siam?" Instead of coming up with hundreds of sites for kids to sift through, Ask Jeeves for Kids comes up with one site to answer their question.

Plus, the answer to every question Jeeves has an answer for has been screened for kid-safe, "G"-rated content. Whether kids need help with homework or they are just curious, Jeeves can be a great help.

Also Worth a Look:

Homework Help
www.startribune.com/stonline/html/special/homework

Kid's Web
www.npac.syr.edu/textbook/kidsweb

Digital Education Network
www.actden.com

My Virtual Reference Desk
www.refdesk.com

CATEGORY: News & Weather
ACTIVITY: Read Custom, Personalized News

CNN Custom News

customnews.cnn.com

CNN Custom News is a free service offered by CNN Interactive. It allows you to customize the news you see, according to your interests. Choose one of the preconfigured profiles, like "Business," "Sports," or "A Little Bit Of Everything." Or build your own profile. In each of several broad categories like World, Business, and Science, you can pick detailed descriptions of the types of stories you want to see. Choose specific countries or regions in World, specific teams in Sports, stock prices and industries in Business, and topics in Science.

Even if you don't customize it, CNN's site is an excellent resource, providing in-depth news and analyses. The site includes a video vault, where you can replay historic moments.

Local Interest:

Gambit Weekly
`www.bestofneworleans.com`

NOLA Live, with the Times Picayune
`www.nolalive.com`

CityBusiness
`www.neworleans.com/citybusiness`

WWL-TV
`www.wwl-tv.com`

Also Worth a Look:

News Index
`www.newsindex.com`

My Yahoo
`my.yahoo.com`

Infoseek News Center
`www.infoseek.com/Topic/news`

Pointcast Network
`www.pointcast.com`

CATEGORY: News & Weather
ACTIVITY: Survive a Hurricane

Storm 99

www.storm99.com

During hurricane season, if you can't get to a television, the next best place to get your storm information is on the Web. That is, until you lose your power. Sites like Storm 99 can help you prepare for a storm, stay informed about a storm's progress, and find out what to do after the storm.

Storm 99 is like a magazine devoted to hurricanes. Satellite and radar images are updated every 15 minutes. Sign up for their e-mail notification service, and they will send you e-mail alerts whenever severe weather is approaching. Storm 99 also has a hurricane shopping list to print, a survival guide, and audio updates in English and Spanish. And for some stunning video and photography, follow the link to Lightening Stalker David O. Stilling, who spends his time chasing storms in his attempt to capture lightening on film.

Also Worth a Look:

National Hurricane Center
`www.nhc.noaa.gov`

CNN Storm Center
`www.cnn.com/WEATHER/storm.center`

American Red Cross Hurricane Center
`www.redcross.org/news/disaster/96/hcane.html`

FEMA
`www.fema.gov/fema/trop.htm`

Other Resources:

Software: Tracking the Eye 5.0 for Windows
`www.gencode.com/hurricane/hurricane.htm`

Lightening Stalker
`www.lightningstalker.com`

CATEGORY: People
ACTIVITY: Finding People

Switchboard

www.switchboard.com

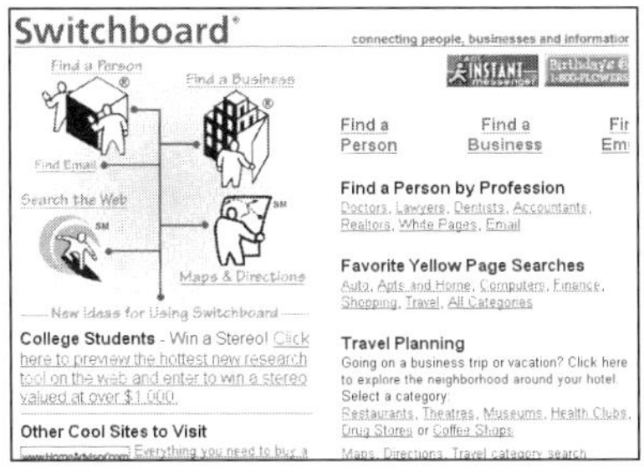

In addition to joining together computers, the Web can also bring together people. You can use the Web to find and contact long-distance friends and family, without expensive phone bills.

Switchboard contains over 1.6 million residential listings and 11 million business listings. Type the name of a friend, family member, or colleague. Unless the number is unlisted, chances are you will find it here.

The sites below can help you find e-mail addresses (even for celebrities), personal Web pages, and mailing addresses. Some will let you do reverse lookups, enabling you to get a name if all you have is a phone number. Locateme.com even allows you to search on a first name, previous address, or a date of birth, which can be very helpful for locating re-married women or the birth parents of adopted children.

Also Worth a Look:

Four11
www.four11.com

WhoWhere
www.whowhere.com

InfoSpace
www.infospace.com

HotBot
www.hotbot.com

The Mining Company's Guide to Personal Home Pages
personalweb.miningco.com

World E-mail Directory
www.worldemail.com

Internet Address Finder
www.iaf.net
locateme.com
www.folksfinder.com

CATEGORY: People
ACTIVITY: Join a Community

Xoom

www.xoom.com

Xoom is an online community that offers free personal home pages, free chat rooms, and free e-mail to its members.

Xoom is divided into communities that serve as neighborhoods, joining together people with similar interests. A charity group might have a home page in the "Organizations" community, while astronomers might discuss heavenly bodies in "Education and Science." With a community for many diverse interests, Xoom offers a place for anyone to meet new friends.

Most online communities offer similar free services. Some (like SeniorNet) cater to older people, while others (like Tripod) are for GenXers. Most are free, but will put ads on your personal home page.

Local Interest:

Yat Chat (NOLA Live with the Times-Picayune)
http://www.nolalive.com/chat/yatchat

The Mining Company's New Orleans Bulletin Board
neworleans.miningco.com/mpboards.html

Also Worth a Look:

AngelFire
www.angelfire.com

GeoCities
www.geocities.com

SeniorNet
www.seniornet.com

TalkCity
www.talkcity.com

Tripod
www.tripod.com

The Well
www.well.com

DejaNews
www.dejanews.com

Category: People
Activity: Send Virtual Greetings

Blue Mountain Arts

www.bluemountainarts.com

Free greeting cards on the Internet have become very popular, and it is no wonder: they are fun to send, they are fun to receive, and they are free.

Blue Mountain Arts offers greeting cards for many occasions, including birthday, sympathy, thank you, and more holidays than you might even know existed (like the Chinese Moon Festival). Many cards are animated and play music.

Once you customize a card and send it, Blue Mountain Arts e-mails your recipient to notify them that a card is waiting. There is no special software required; as long as your recipient has a Web browser, she will be able to see the card.

Local Interest:

E-Cards from the Big Easy
`www.nolalive.com/nola_cards`

Also Worth a Look:

Regards.com
`www.regards.com`

123Greetings
`www.123greetings.com`

LoveCards: Love and Romance in a Postcard
`www.lovecards.com`

Activegrams
`www.activegrams.com`

Easyriders Postcards on the Edge
`www.easyriders.com/postcards`

Other Resources:

Never Forget (personal reminder software)
`neverforget.com`

CATEGORY: People
ACTIVITY: Send Instant Messages

ICQ

www.icq.com

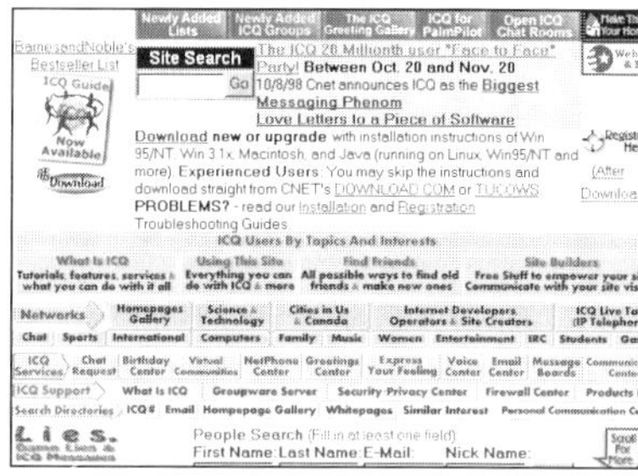

ICQ, pronounced "I seek you," is a novel way of keeping in touch with your buddies on the Web. Once you and your friends join and identify each other on your "buddy" list, you are in business. You can find out who is on the Web when you are and send them instant messages that pop up on screen, or you can open a private chat window. You can play games together or send files.

ICQ helps you make new friends as well by matching random people up to chat. Or, hook up with new friends according to interest or affiliation.

Also Worth a Look:

AOL Messenger
`www.aol.com/aim`

Ding!
`www.ding.com`

Ichat
`www.ichat.com`

PageNet (send a message to an alphanumeric pager)
`www.pagenet.com/sendpage`

Pagoo (toll-free Internet voice mailbox)
`www.pagoo.com`

PAL: Personal Access List
`talk.excite.com/communities/excite/pal`

PeopleLink
`www.peoplelink.com`

Category: Sports
Activity: Follow Your Team

ESPN Sportszone: Saints Clubhouse

espn.sportszone.com/nfl/clubhouses/nor.html

Now that football season is in full swing, it's time to join in the action... on the Internet. If you can't get enough news, stats, and highlights, just head to the Web.

ESPN SportsZone, one of the most popular sites on the Web, hosts the Saints Clubhouse. All the latest news about the team, interviews, and team standings are here. The game schedule links to the other team's pages, so you can read up on the opponents. Plus, the schedule links to Ticketmaster Online, so you can purchase tickets to all of the away games over the Internet.

Local Interest:

NFL Saints Page
www.nfl.com/saints

CNN/SI Saints Page
cnnsi.com/football/nfl/teams/saints

Zephyrs
www.zephyrsbaseball.com

Also Worth a Look:

Minor League Baseball
www.minorleaguebaseball.com

FASTBALL (Major League Baseball)
www.fastball.com

NBA.com
www.nba.com

NFL.com
www.nfl.com

ESPN SportsZone
www.sportszone.com

CATEGORY: Sports
ACTIVITY: Talk to Other Fans

Gridiron Grumblings

www.gridirongrumblings.com

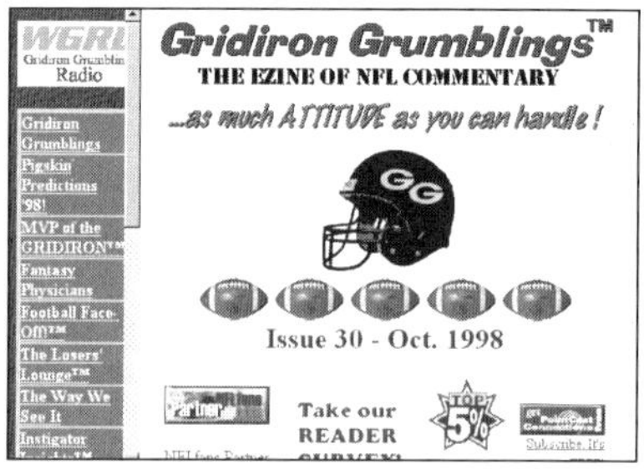

If Sunday's action just wouldn't be the same without Monday morning's quarterbacking, then you can find some new friends at Gridiron Grumblings. Billed as "The E-Zine of NFL Commentary," this site is filled with predictions, analyses, and complaints from armchair quarterbacks everywhere.

"Loser's Lounge" the sports Hall of Shame, singles out a player each month to bash. The Saints have the dubious distinction of being the only entire team featured.

The sites below all host areas for fans to get together. There are newsgroups devoted to every pro football team.

Local Interest:

NFL Saints Page
www.nfl.com/saints

DejaNews (subscribe to the newsgroup alt.sports.football.pro.no-saints)
www.dejanews.com

Also Worth a Look:

Mining Company NFL Chat
profootball.miningco.com/mpchat.htm

ESPN Chat
chat2-espnet.sportszone.com/chat/chat.dll?template=SZ_NFL

Monday Night Football Chat
www.abcmnf.com/skybox/chat_intro.html

WBS NFL Chat
www.wbs.net

CATEGORY: Travel
ACTIVITY: Buy Airline Tickets

Expedia

expedia.msn.com

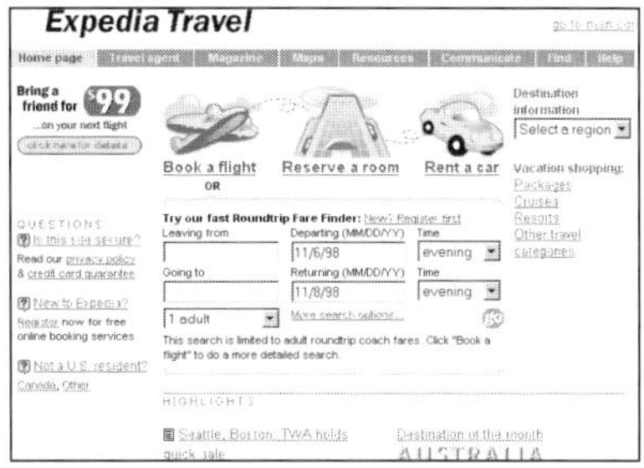

Expedia lets you be your own travel agent. By typing in the time and date of your trip, and the destination, you can check several airlines at once for the perfect flight. Pick the exact time of departure, choose a direct or connecting flight, and even select your own seat assignment from a map of the plane.

Several sites offer a free e-mail notification service. Specify a destination, and you will be notified if the fare changes.

Check the individual airline sites also. Often, they will post Internet-only specials and last-minute deals. And check the Southwest Airlines site, since their flight information is generally not available through Expedia.

Also Worth a Look:

Travelocity
www.travelocity.com

Preview Travel
www.previewtravel.com

Priceline
www.priceline.com

Southwest Airlines
www.iflyswa.com

American Airlines
www.aa.com

Last Minute Airfare Deals
www.lowairfares.com/lastlow.htm

Continental Airlines CO.OL
www.cooltravelassistant.com

TWA
www.twa.com

United Airlines E Fares
www.ual.com

CATEGORY: Travel
ACTIVITY: Plan a Vacation

Fodor's Travel Online

www.fodors.com

For recommendations on where to stay, what to see, and where to dine on your trip, visit Fodor's. The famed guidebook publisher keeps a database of hotel and restaurant reviews from around the world.

If you are going to one of Fodor's 76 international cities, you can build a personalized travel guide. First answer questions about where you are going and what types of hotels, restaurants, sightseeing, and travel information you would like to see. Fodor's will put together a personalized travel guide. You can then print the guide to take on the road. As complete as it is, it might even help you out when you are trying to use a public phone in Helsinki.

Also Worth a Look:

The Travel Corner
www.travelcorner.com

Frommer's Encyclopedia of Travel
www.mcp.com/frommers

Traveler.Net
www.traveler.net

Atevo Travel
www.atevo.com

World Travel Guide
www.wtgonline.com/start.html

TraveLoco
www.traveloco.com

Las Vegas Convention & Visitors Authority
www.lasvegas24hours.com

The Mining Company's Travel Hub
www.miningco.com/travel

Category: Travel
Activity: Print a Map

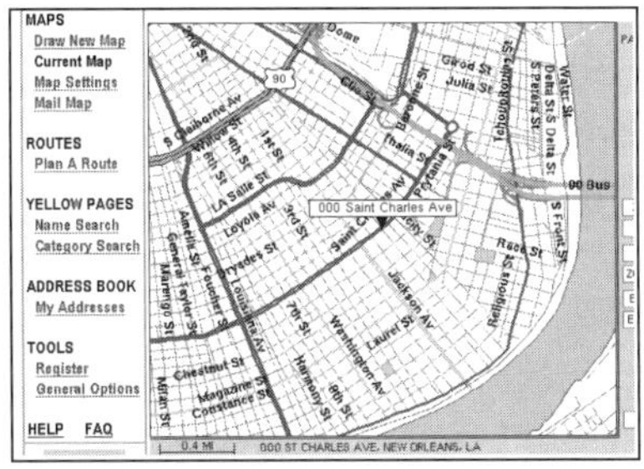

Maps On Us

www.mapsonus.com

If only your car had Internet access. Maps On Us works on a simple concept: type an address, and get a map of the area. Tell it where you are and where you wish to go, and it will give you detailed driving directions, whether you are going across town or across the country. Print the map top take with you, or e-mail it to all your party guests.

Maps On Us combines with the Switchboard "yellow pages" directory. Once you have located an address, you can identify nearby businesses like shopping centers, grocery stores, movie theaters, transportation, and attractions. This feature is particularly useful when you are buying a new house or traveling.

Also Worth a Look:

MapQuest
www.mapquest.com

Rand McNally
www.randmcnally.com

Yahoo! Maps
maps.yahoo.com

MapBlast!
www.mapblast.com

Glossary of Internet Terms

The Internet comes with a whole new language. Often, hearing words you don't fully understand can make your Internet experience harder than it needs to be.

Use this section whenever you come across an unfamiliar word, either within this book, on the Web itself, or in a newspaper or magazine article. The terms in this section are all explained in English. You can also read over these terms to build your Internet vocabulary and impress your friends and family!

But first, learn how to say some common symbols out loud:

Symbol	Pronounced	Where you might see it
!	"bang"	old e-mail addresses
@	"at"	e-mail addresses
~	"till-duh" (spelled tilde)	some personal Web addresses
/	"forward slash"	most Web addresses
.	"dot"	most Web addresses, e-mail addreses, and the names of newsgroups on Usenet
*	"asterisk"	used in search engines as a wildcard

A

Adobe Acrobat

A free program from Adobe that allows you view and print PDF files, which are common on the Web. You can download Acrobat Reader, free, from `www.adobe.com`. (See also **PDF file**)

access provider (See **Internet Service Provider**)

acronym

A word used as a shorthand for a series of other words. Often, acronyms are used in e-mail, chat rooms, and message boards to save space and time. Some of the more common acronyms are listed below:

AFK	**Away From Keyboard**
BFN	**Bye For Now**
BRB	**Be Right Back**
BTDTGTS	**Been There, Done That, Got the T-Shirt**
BTW	**By The Way**
CUL8R	**See You Later**
FTF	**Face-to-Face**
FWIW	**For What It's Worth**
FYI	**For Your Information**
GAL	**Get A Life**
G	**Grin**
GG	**(big) Grin**
HTH	**Hope This Helps**
IAE	**In Any Event**

IANAL	**I Am Not A Lawyer**
ILY	**I Love You**
IMHO	**In My Humble Opinion**
IMNSHO	**In My Not So Humble Opinion**
IRL	**In Real Life**
ISWYM	**I See What You Mean**
LOL	**Laughing Out Loud**
NRN	**No Reply Necessary**
OIC	**Oh, I See!**
OOTB	**Out Of The Box (brand new)**
OTOH	**On The Other Hand**
PDA	**Public Display of Affection**
ROTFL	**Rolling On The Floor Laughing**
RSN	**Real Soon Now (often sarcastic)**
RTFM	**Read The Frigging Manual**
TIA	**Thanks In Advance**
TTYL	**Talk To You Later**

Note: Usually, acronyms that denote an emotion are typed between the symbols for less-than and greater-than (for example, <LOL> stands for "laughing out loud"). Acronyms that are short for a phrase are typed alone (for example, TTFN for "ta ta for now").

ActiveX

ActiveX controls are small programs which are sometimes downloaded along with Web pages. They can control things like animation on a Web page. ActiveX is Microsoft's answer to Sun's Java. See also **Java**.

address

On the Internet, an address can refer to:

1. where you would send e-mail
2. where you can find a Web page
3. a computer's unique location on the Internet (See IP address)

America Online (AOL)

The largest of the commercial online service providers. Because of its ease of use and extensive advertising, millions of newcomers to the Internet choose AOL as their introduction to the Internet. Besides providing Internet access, AOL offers member services such as news, travel services, special interest areas, and chat rooms.

animated GIF

A picture on a Web page that moves or changes. An animated GIF can be a small cartoon that loops continuously, or perhaps a dog that runs across the screen and stops. These are often used on Web sites to add some pizzazz without slowing down the time it takes for the page to load on your computer.

anonymous FTP (See **FTP**)

anti-virus software

A program that scans your hard drive, as well as any programs you download from the Internet or install from floppy disks, for known viruses. Anti-virus software vendors provide updates as new viruses are identified.

application

Software designed for a specific purpose. For example, a word processor program like Microsoft Word, an e-mail program like Eudora, and a browser like Netscape Navigator are all examples of different applications. The terms "software," "program," and "application" are generally used as synonyms. Applications depend on your computer's operating system to function. Sometimes shortened to "app."

ASCII

Pronounced out loud, it rhymes with "passkey." ASCII is the set of numbers, letters, and symbols that are found on your keyboard. ASCII files (also called "plain text" files) are the most common type of text files on the Internet, because every type of computer can read them. They don't contain any special formatting, like bold or italics. Simple word processing software (like Notepad in Windows) creates ASCII files, but any word processing program (such as Word) can read them. (ASCII stands for American Standard Code for Information Interchange.)

attached file (attachment)

A file (such as a picture, a word processor document, or even a software program) that is sent along with an e-mail message.

B

backbone

The main "pipes" of the Internet, where most of the information is transmitted. In general, government agencies, giant telecommunications companies, and large Internet Service Providers maintain the backbone. Everyone else, including businesses, universities, and smaller ISPs, connect to them.

bandwidth

If you think of the Internet as the Information Superhighway, then think of bandwidth as how many lanes of traffic it can handle. Bandwidth describes how much information that can be sent over a connection at one time. In the past, the Internet had more than enough bandwidth to handle the traffic. Now, millions of people have come online. And complex information like video, audio, and virtual reality is adding to the problem. More people accessing more complex information means more traffic jams on the Internet.

baud

The speed of a modem (how fast it can send and receive information) used to be measured in baud. This term is being replaced now by bps (bits per second). Although they are often confused, baud and bps are two different measurements. (See **bps**)

bcc:

You'll see this in your e-mail program. Short for "blind carbon copy," it is used to send a copy of the e-mail message to someone without the knowledge of the person to whom you're addressing the e-mail. (See **e-mail, cc:**)

beta

Software that has not officially been released. A beta version of a program is one step away from the final version. The creators of the program want as many people as possible to use the program. This way, they can find bugs in the software and get feedback before it is released commercially. Beta software is distributed free, and does not come with a warranty or instructions. Beta versions usually have an expiration date, after which you will have a chance to buy the final, commercial version. A beta version is a good way to see if you would like the final version, and it often gives you the opportunity to let your opinions be heard on the program. (See **shareware**, **freeware**)

BinHex

Used on the Macintosh, BinHex is a software utility that encodes files so they can travel over the Internet. When you download a file, or if someone sends you a file as an e-mail attachment, it will often have the extension .hqx. Browsers like Netscape and e-mail programs like Eudora have built-in BinHex decoders, or you can download one off the Internet.

bit

The smallest amount of information a computer can understand. You can think of a bit as a switch that is either on ("1") or off ("0"). All of the information a computer handles, whether it is text, video, audio, or virtual reality, can be broken down into a long series of bits. Eight bits in a row form a byte. Every letter, number, and symbol on your keyboard is represented by a byte. By the way, half of a byte (4 bits) is called a nibble.

A kilobyte (KB) is slightly more than 1,000 bytes (to be precise, 2 to the 10th power, or 1,024 bytes).

A megabyte (MB) is slightly more than 1,000,000 bytes (2 to the 20th power, or 1,048,576).

A gigabyte is slightly more than 1,000,000,000 (one billion) bytes (2 to the 30th power, or 1,073,741,824).

bookmark

It's tough to find what you are looking for on the Web. It can be even tougher to get back to something you saw before. If you find a site you think you will want to visit again, most browsers let you set a bookmark. The bookmarks you set serve as shortcuts to your favorite sites. Internet Explorer calls them "Favorites," but they serve the same purpose.

Boolean

This term refers to using the terms "AND" and "OR" to help you search for information on the Web. For example, you might be looking for a Web page that contains both of the words "kids AND school." Or, you might be looking for a page that contains either "boys OR girls." Boolean logic refers to using the two "operators," AND and OR, to help you in your search.

boot

To start up or reset a computer. A cold boot occurs when a computer is turned on with the power switch. A warm boot occurs when a computer that is already on is restarted.

bps

Short for "bits per second", bps refers to the speed a modem can transmit and receive information. One kilobit per second (kbps) equals 1,000 bps. Common modem speeds are 28.8 Kbps and 56 Kbps.

browser

Software that allows you to see and hear the information on the World Wide Web. Simply put, a browser displays a Web page on your computer screen. Currently, the two most popular browsers are Microsoft's Internet Explorer, and Netscape's Navigator. You can usually get these, free of charge, from your ISP or from the Web itself.

bug

An error in software that can cause unexpected or unusual behavior. During testing, programmers attempt to find and fix all of the bugs. However, some bugs are not caught until after the program is released to the public. Companies often distribute software "patches" that people can download to fix bugs in software.

byte (See **bit**)

C

cache

An area of your computer's memory or hard drive that "remembers" Web pages you've visited recently. You may have noticed that when you return to a Web page you have already seen, it loads much more quickly than it did the first time. That's because your computer didn't have to request that information from the Internet again; it just pulled the page out of the cache. Pages are only stored in cache temporarily; when you close your browser, the cache is cleared out. For tips on using your cache to speed up your Web surfing, see *"Getting the Most Out of Your Browser."*

cc:

You'll see this in your e-mail program. Short for "carbon copy," it is used to send a copy of the e-mail message to someone else (See **e-mail**, **bcc:**)

CD-ROM

Short for "Compact Disk - Read Only Memory." A CD-ROM disk stores about 600 megabytes of information (approximately the equivalent of an entire set of encyclopedias). A CD-ROM drive reads information from a disk.

CPU (central processing unit) (See **processor**)

channel

1. On the Web, a Web site that automatically sends up-to-date information to another Web site or to your desktop (See **push technology**)

2. In Internet Relay Chat (IRC), a specific chat room.

chat

A typed conversation between two or more people, in real time, over the Internet. In a chat room, the messages you type are shown instantly to every other member of the chat room. Messages typed by other people are shown immediately to you. Most chat rooms use a protocol called IRC (Internet Relay Chat). For chat rooms on many topics, try `www.talkcity.com`.

click

Pressing a mouse button. A "left click" means the leftmost button on a two- or three-button mouse is pressed. A "right click" means the rightmost button is pressed. To "shift click" means to hold down the "Shift" key on the keyboard while clicking the mouse button.

client

A computer that requests information from another computer (a **"server"**). For example, when you visit a page on the Web, your browser acts as a client, requesting a page from a server somewhere on the Web. The server sends you the page you requested, and the browser displays it on your screen.

Communicator (See **Netscape Navigator**)

compression

Technology that reduces the size of a file or group of files. Several files can be compressed into one smaller file. The smaller file can be transmitted over the Internet faster. The files must be uncompressed before they are used. (See **zipped file**)

cookie

A small file that is stored on your hard drive by a Web site with the help of your browser. A cookie usually contains information about you which helps the Web site personalize your experience. See *"Staying Smart, Safe, and Secure."*

counter

A program on a Web page that keeps track of the number of people who visit the site. The counter displays a total number of visits on the page, for everyone to see. For free counters for use on your personal home page, see `www.digitmania.com`.

cyber

A prefix used to describe something or someone as part of the computer age. For example, the Internet is often referred to as Cyberspace. A person who on the Internet is called a Cybercitizen.

Cyberspace

A synonym for the Internet.

D

demo

A scaled-down version of software designed to show users what a program is about. For example, a game demo might include only the first few levels. Read the description of the program carefully to determine if it is worth the time to download. Demo versions can be a good way to find out if you would enjoy the full version, which can cost anywhere from $40 up to several hundreds of dollars.

dial-up

A temporary connection between two computers, established over a telephone line.

digital cash

Electronic money that can be spent over the Internet or stored on cards similar to credit cards. Digital cash can be spent in very small denominations, such as a tenth of a cent.

digital video (See **DVD**)

DVD (digital versatile disk)

A new disk which is expected to replace the CD-ROM in the next couple of years. A DVD can hold up to 17 gigabytes of information, including video and audio. That is about 28 times the amount a CD-ROM can hold, and more than enough to play back an entire movie. DVD players can also read regular CD-ROMs.

discussion board (See **message board**)

diskette

Usually this term refers to the 3.5" plastic disk used to store files. It is sometimes referred to as a **floppy disk**, since the actual disk (inside the plastic cover) is a flexible magnetic medium. A 3.5" diskette can store up to 1.44 megabytes (MB) of information.

domain name

The location of a computer (or group of computers) on the Internet. Domain names look similar to this: `muppets.com`. Together with the name of a specific computer, a domain name can take you to a location on the Internet. For example, `www.muppets.com` would point to the Muppets' site. Typing `kermit.muppets.com` might take you to Kermit's computer, where you would see a different Web site.

Domain names must be registered with InterNIC (usually your ISP can do this for you). To find out who owns a particular domain name, or to find out if a domain name is available for you to register, visit `rs.internic.net`.

DNS (Domain Name System)

A system that allows Web site addresses to be words instead of numbers. A Web site address (also called an IP address) is actually a series of numbers and dots, like this: `123.45.6.78`. Instead of remembering those numbers, you would type words like this: `www.example.com`. The DNS system would match those words to the correct IP address and bring you to the Web site. (See **domain name**, **IP address**)

DOS (Disk Operating System)

An early operating system installed on personal computers. DOS requires the user to type in commands to run software. It was considered more difficult to use than today's graphical operating systems, like Windows (for the PC) and System 7 (for the Mac).

download

To copy a file from a computer on the Internet to your own computer. Software files are transferred using a **protocol** called **FTP**. When you download a file, your browser will first ask you where on your hard drive you want to save the file. Web pages are downloaded using a protocol called **HTTP**. Download is the opposite of **upload**.

E

e-cash (See **digital cash**)

e-mail

Electronic mail. E-mail was one of the first uses of the Internet and is still the most popular.

e-mail address

The location where e-mail is sent to a particular individual. E-mail addresses are usually made up of a user name, the "at" sign (@), and the user's domain name. For example: `kermit@muppets.com`.

emoticon (See **smiley**)

e-zine

Short for "electronic magazine." Since the Web is such an inexpensive method of publishing information, hundreds of e-zines exist on many obscure subjects. For a list of e-zines, visit the E-Zine Database at `www.pol2000.com/ezines.html`.

F

FAQ

Short for "Frequently Asked Questions" and pronounced "fack." A FAQ is a document created to answer the questions of a beginner. FAQs exist for every topic from *South Park* to fertilizer.

favorites (See **bookmark**)

file

A collection of data stored on a computer, with its own unique name. A file can contain a program (like a word processor) or a document (like the novel you jut wrote in your word processor).

FTP (file transfer protocol)

The method by which computers can send files to one another over the Internet. (See **download**)

flame

A message posted to a public bulletin board or e-mailed that is insulting or strongly critical. When a series of insulting messages are exchanged publicly, it is referred to as a "flame war."

floppy disk (See **diskette**)

forum

An area of a Web site where particular topics are discussed. This is typically a message board where members post messages for the entire group to read.

frames

The division of a Web page into separate, independent sections. For example, a page might have a menu in a frame on the left side of the page. Clicking on a choice in the menu might bring up a file in the frame on the right side of the page.

freeware

Software available for you to download and use, free of charge. While some freeware is excellent, remember that often, you get what you pay for. (See **shareware**)

G

gigabyte (See **bit**)

GIF

Stands for Graphics Interchange Format. Pronounced with either a hard or soft G ("ghif" or "jif"). One of the two most common graphic file formats on the Web. (See also **JPEG**)

H

hard drive (hard disk)

The main storage device within a computer where **files** are stored. Today's computers typically come with several **gigabytes** of storage space.

helper app

An application that your browser uses to show you a file type that it can't display on its own. Similar to **plug-ins**, except that helper apps use their own separate window (plug-ins use the browser window, so they look like part of the browser). (See **plug-in**)

HTML (Hypertext Markup Language)

The language used to write Web pages. HTML is actually a collection of "tags" which tell your browser how to display a Web page. HTML tags determine the size and color of the words on your screen, where the graphics are displayed, and what pages the hypertext is linked to. You can take a look at the HTML for any page on the Web by clicking on the "View" menu in your browser and selecting "View Document Source."

HTTP (Hypertext Transfer Protocol)

The protocol used by the Web to send and receive HTML files (Web pages). You will sometimes see this in front of a Web address (for example, `http://www.site.com`), but generally you do not have to type it into your browser.

hyperlink

A connection between one Web page and another. Any object on page, whether it is words, a picture, or an animation, can be hyperlinked to any other page on the Web. When you click on a hyperlinked object and go to another Web page, you have followed a hyperlink.

hypertext

Text that links to another document, such as a Web page. Jumping from page to page (and site to site) on the Web is as easy as clicking on hypertext with a mouse. Hypertext is usually (but not always) underlined so you can recognize it. Pictures, videos, and other objects can also be **hyperlinks** to other Web pages. (See **hyperlink**)

Hypertext Markup Language (See **HTML**)

I

icon

A small picture that represents a file or software program. Usually, you can open the file or run the program by pointing the mouse cursor at the icon and double-clicking (pressing the left mouse button twice quickly).

IRC (Internet Relay Chat)

A system for "talking" to other people in real time, online. Chat groups (also called channels) exist on many different topics. Several people can participate in the group at once; when one person types a message, the entire group sees it immediately.

Information Superhighway

A synonym for the **Internet**. (See **Internet**)

Internet

A network of computers all over the world which communicate with each other using common **protocols**. Beginning as a military network called ARPANet in 1969, the Internet later expanded to include universities and now businesses. It includes many services, such as **e-mail**, **chat**, **file transfer**, and the **World Wide Web**. The Internet is often called the **Net**, the **Information Superhighway**, or **Cyberspace**.

Internet Explorer

Currently, one of the two most popular Web **browsers** (with **Netscape Navigator**). The browser is available, free, at `www.microsoft.com`.

Internet Service Provider (ISP)

A company that provides access to the Internet, usually for a monthly fee. Local and national companies are available. Generally, you use your modem to dial in to the ISP's modem, and they will give you direct access to all of the Internet services. Commercial online services like America Online and Compuserve also provide a gateway to the Internet, but more experienced users generally prefer direct access through an ISP.

InterNIC

The organization that registers and keeps track of all the **domain names** on the Web. To find out who owns a particular domain name, or to find out if a domain name is available for you to register, visit `rs.internic.net`.

IP (Internet Protocol)

The means by which all computers on the Internet find each other. Whenever you look at a Web page or send e-mail, you are sending information across the Internet from one computer to another. Internet Protocol handles the address part of that information, making sure the information gets to the right place. (IP is part of **TCP/IP**, the protocol that allows all the computers of the Internet to talk to each other.) (See **IP Address** and **TCP/IP**)

IP address

Every computer on the Internet has an IP address, just as every building in the real world has a postal address. IP addresses consist of four sets of numbers separated by periods (for example, `111.22.333.4`). When it comes to remembering so many numbers, human beings have a harder time than computers do. So IP addresses are usually written as domain names. For example, an IP address like this: `255.242.27.44` might be written like this: `greenpeace.org`.

J

Java

No, it's not just a drink. Java is a computer language created by Sun Microsytems. Software written in Java can run on any type of computer, which makes it ideal for the Internet. (Software written in most other languages only work on a specific type of computer, such as a Mac or a Windows PC.) Programs written in Java can be full-featured applications (like a spreadsheet) or small **"applets"** designed to add functionality to a Web page (like a stock ticker that scrolls across your home page). Although they sound similar, Java is not the same as **JavaScript**.

JavaScript

A scripting language, created by Netscape, which Web page designers use to add simple functionality to a Web page. For example, if you've ever seen a button on a Web page change colors when you moved your mouse cursor over it, chances are that was done with JavaScript. JavaScript is much simpler than **Java** but not as powerful.

JPEG

Stands for Joint Photographic Experts Group and is pronounced "jay-peg." One of the two most common graphic file formats on the Web. JPEG files are most commonly digital photographs. The file name usually has the suffix `.jpg`. (See **GIF**)

K

K56flex

A modem that can transfer data at a top speed of 56 Kpbs. This is one of the standards for the fastest modems currently available (the other is x2). K56flex and x2 are not compatible with each other; so if you buy a 56 Kbps modem, make sure your ISP can support the one you choose.

Kbps (See **bps**)

keyword

A word that lets a search engine know what you are looking for. The more unique and specific your keywords are, the more successful your search will be. For example, avoid common words like "baseball," use instead unique words like "New Orleans Zephyrs." See *"Finding What You Need."*

kilobyte (KB) (See **bit**)

L

list server

A program that automatically handles subscriptions for a mailing list. A list server handles new subscription requests and cancellations, and sends new messages to the entire list of subscribers. (The two most common list server programs are ListServ and MajorDomo.)

live cam (See **Webcam**)

logon (login)

Signing on to a remote computer. Generally, you will need a user ID and a password to log in. Many Web sites require you to register for access to the entire site and will give you a user ID and password to use.

lurker

Someone who visits a chat room or Internet newsgroup without participating. A lurker will read what other people are saying and not speak up. Far from being rude, lurking is actually recommended, especially if you are new to a newsgroup. Lurking is a good way to get to know the rules and the way things are done before you jump into the conversation.

M

mailing list

A group of people who receive a regular e-mail message on a particular topic. Mailing lists exist on over 30,000 different subjects. Signing up for a mailing list is usually free. You can find a list of mailing lists at `catalog.com/vivian/interest-group-search.html`.

megahertz (Mhz)

A measure of the speed of a computer's **processor**. The higher the number, the faster the computer. Today's computers come in processor speeds of 400 Mhz or more.

megabyte (MB) (See **bit**)

memory

A temporary holding place for information that your computer needs to be able to access quickly. Memory usually refers to RAM (Random Access Memory). Information stored in memory is lost when the computer is turned off. (Be careful not to confuse memory with storage areas like the hard drive. Information stored on the hard drive does not disappear when the computer is turned off.) (See **RAM**)

message board

Any online "bulletin board" that allows you to post messages on a particular topic and read messages posted by others. (See **newsgroups**)

microprocessor (See **processor**)

mirror site

An exact copy of a Web site placed at another location. Often, a popular site will create a mirror site to ease traffic congestion. For example, Netscape has placed mirror sites in different countries around the world for people to download the Navigator browser.

MMX

Technology within a Pentium **processor** designed to run multimedia applications faster. Newer software includes much more video, audio, and graphics then ever before. MMX technology helps speed up all that by handling the multimedia more efficiently.

modem

A modem is the device that allows your computer to communicate with other computers, using a standard telephone line. Modems are rated by their speed, measured in **Kbps**. The larger the number, the faster the modem can send and receive **bits** of information.

MSIE

Short for Microsoft Internet Explorer. (See **Internet Explorer**)

multimedia

A mix of text, sound, still and animated images, and/or video. Multimedia computers are capable of displaying all of these different elements.

N

Navigator (See **Netscape Navigator**)

Netscape Navigator (Netscape Communicator)

Currently, one of the two most popular Web **browsers** (with **Internet Explorer**). The newest Netscape browser is called Communicator. The browser is available, free, at `www.netscape.com`.

Net (or 'net')

A synonym for the Internet. (See **Internet**)

netiquette

Short for "network etiquette." The set of rules that govern behavior on the Internet. See *"Sending and Receiving E-mail"* for a rundown on e-mail netiquette rules. (See **flame**)

network

A group of computers connected together. Computers that are networked together can share information with each other. The **Internet** is the largest of all networks; it connects many other networks together throughout the world.

newbie

Someone who is new to the Internet or to technology in general.

newsgroup

A message board on Usenet. (See **message board**, **Usenet**)

NNTP (Network News Transfer Protocol)

The **protocol** used to read and post messages on Usenet newsgroups.

O

offline

Not currently connected to the Internet.

online

Currently connected to the Internet.

operating system

The software that controls the most basic functions of the computer, such as the processor, memory, mouse, and keyboard. Common operating systems include Windows (for the PC) and System 7 (for the Mac).

P

packet

A small chunk of data sent over the Internet. All information (whether it is e-mail, a Web page, or a picture) is broken up into packets before it is sent across the Internet. Each packet contains the address of the final destination, and they may each take a different route. When all of the packets reach their final destination, they are reassembled into the original file.

Pentium

The **processor** used in many personal computers. The Pentium Pro adds extra cache memory for the processor to use, speeding up its operations. The Pentium II adds even more cache memory and includes MMX technology. (See **MMX**)

page (See **Web page**)

PDF (Portable Document Format)

A type of file commonly used on the Internet to display magazine articles, brochures, and user manuals. Your browser can't read these files without help; you must have the Acrobat Reader program to view and print PDF files. Acrobat Reader is free to download from Adobe's site, `www.adobe.com`.

PGP (Pretty Good Privacy)

Software that encrypts e-mail, protecting it from being read by anyone except the intended recipient. See "*Sending and Receiving E-mail.*" PGP is free and available at `www.pgpi.com`.

platform

Describes the type of computer and operating system. A PC with Windows 95 is a common type of platform. A Macintosh is another.

plug-in

A program that adds extra capability to your browser. Plug-ins install directly into your browser and allow you to see and hear things that your browser can't play on its own. Usually if you visit a Web site that requires a certain plug-in, they will provide you with a link to download the plug-in you need. Plug-ins you're likely to come across include **Shockwave** (audio, video, and animation), **RealAudio** (more audio and video), and **Acrobat** (documents that look like printed books or brochures). (See **helper app**)

POP (Point of Presence)

A connection to the Internet. Your Internet Service Provider has at least one POP. Often an ISP will set up a POP in another city to help its customers avoid long-distance telephone charges. For example, if your ISP is headquartered in New Orleans but has a POP in Chicago, you will be able to make a local connection while in the Chicago area.

PPP (Point to Point Protocol)

The **protocol** used by your modem to allow your computer to communicate with your ISP's server.

post

A message sent to a public place, like a newsgroup, where it can be read by many other people. (Post can be used as a noun or a verb. You can post a message to a newsgoup. The message itself is also called a post.)

postmaster

The name of the person in charge of e-mail for a Web site. Generally, if you send an e-mail message to `postmaster@anysite.com`, it should be received by a human being.

processor

The main chip that controls a computer's functions.

program

A set of instructions for the computer to follow. Programs are also called **software** and **applications**.

protocol

A special set of rules and conventions that govern how different kinds of computers and software communicate over a network. There are two main protocols on the Internet: **TCP** (Transmission Control Protocol) and **IP** (Internet Protocol).

Q

Quicktime

A multimedia technology that combines text, sound, animation, and video into a single file. Quicktime files usually have the extension `.qt`, `.mov`, or `.moov`. A special Quicktime player is required to view the files. You can download one at Apple's site: `www.apple.com/quicktime`

R

RAM (Random Access Memory)

A temporary holding place for information that your computer needs to be able to access quickly. Information stored in RAM is lost when the computer is turned off.

Computers store information in RAM while running programs. This is because accessing information from RAM is quicker than reading it from the hard drive. So a computer with more RAM is able to work faster. Computers typically come with 32 or 64 megabytes of RAM installed, and more can be added later.

RealAudio

A plug-in which allows you to hear CD-quality audio over your Internet connection. The plug-in software is available, free, at RealNetwork's web site,
`www.real.com`.

S

search engine

A Web site that allows you to find pages throughout the Web by typing in keywords. A search engine uses an automated software agent, called a "spider," which crawls from site to site, cataloging the words it finds in a huge database. When you type in a keyword, the search engine looks through its database and returns a list of pages that included your keyword. One popular search engine is Alta Vista, at
`www.altavista.digital.com`.

self-extracting file

Often, software downloaded from the Internet has been compressed into an `.exe` file. These files are called self-extracting because they will decompress themselves once you double-click on them. (See **compression**)

server

A computer that sends information to other computers (a client). Generally, since the Internet never closes, servers are connected and running 24 hours a day, seven days a week. Just to confuse you, the software that is installed on the computer is also called a server. (See **client**)

service provider (See **Internet Service Provider**)

shareware

Software available for you to "try before you buy." You can download shareware at no cost, and try it out for a trial period. If you like the software and want to continue using it after the trial period, you are asked to pay a registration fee. Once you register the software, you get access to technical support, documentation, and sometimes extra features. If you don't plan to continue using it, you are expected to delete it. You can find a great deal of shareware at `www.shareware.com`. (See **freeware**)

Shockwave

A program by Macromedia that can add animation and interactivity to a Web site. (See **shocked**)

sig (See **signature file**)

site (See **Web site**)

Shocked

A Web site that uses Macromedia's Shockwave technology. Web sites that use Shockwave can look more like a CD-ROM. They can be more interactive, respond to your mouse faster and give you more feedback on what to do next. Or, they can play back a short movie. Compared to a normal Web site, a Shocked site has a lot more pizzazz, but might be much slower to appear. To view a Shocked site, you will need the free plug-in available at `www.macromedia.com/shockwave`.

signature file

A few lines attached to the end of an e-mail which "signs" the message. Signatures usually contain your name, contact information, company name, or your motto. (See *"Sending and Receiving E-mail."*)

SMTP

Stands for Simple Mail Transfer Protocol. The **protocol** that allows for the sending and receiving of e-mail.

smiley

Little sideways smiley faces and other faces drawn with keyboard symbols. Smileys exist because it is so easy to misunderstand an e-mail message. A smiley can let your reader know that you are just kidding, or being sarcastic, or are upset. Below is a list of some common smileys. Tilt your head to the left to see them correctly.

:-) basic smiley
;-) winking smiley
:-(sad
:-D big smile
:-O surprised
:-P sticking your tongue out
8-) smiley with glasses
0:-) angel
:-[vampire
(:)-) scuba diver
(-: left-handed smiley
:-{) smiley with a moustache
*:o) clown smiley
:-# smiley with braces
>:-> really sarcastic smiley

snail mail

Refers to regular postal mail. (Postal mail moves at a snail's pace compared to e-mail.)

software

A set of instructions that allows a computer to perform tasks. (Hardware refers to the physical parts of a computer, like the disk drive and the processor. Hardware requires software before it can do anything useful.) Software is packaged on CD-ROMs or floppy disks, or it can be downloaded from the Internet. Software is also referred to as **programs** or **applications**.

source

The **HTML** behind the Web page you are viewing. (See **HTML**)

spam

Junk e-mail. Bulk e-mail is very inexpensive to send compared to traditional bulk mail. This has made it popular among some businesses who send out unsolicited mass e-mail messages and post messages across several newsgroups, without regard to the relevance of the message to the newsgroup topic. Spam is considered a serious breach of **netiquette**. (In case you are curious, spam gets its name from a Monty Python sketch.)

spider

Software that crawls on the Web (get it?) to gather information about Web sites and the information they contain. Spiders are generally used by indexes, like Alta Vista, to automatically keep track of new and changed sites.

SSL (Secure Sockets Layer)

The protocol that allows for secure transactions over the Web. SSL technology is used to protect sensitive information like credit card numbers and Social Security numbers as they are sent across the Internet. (See *"Staying Smart, Safe, and Secure."*)

surf

To explore the Web without a specific goal. Surfing the Web is similar to channel surfing with a TV remote.

T

TCP/IP

The **protocol**, or language, that all of the computers on the Internet speak (regardless of what country they are in). Stands for Transmission Control Protocol/Internet Protocol. The first part, **TCP**, handles breaking information (like a Web page or an e-mail message) into small pieces for the journey over the Internet and assembling it back together once it reaches its destination. The second part, **IP**, handles the addressing of the message, making sure that each piece of the information gets to the right place.

Telnet

A **protocol** that allows you to log on to a remote computer, just as if it was sitting on your desk. You might use Telnet to access the computerized card catalog at the library.

thread

A series of messages (usually on a message board) covering a particular topic. When several people post messages to each other on one topic, it is similar to a conversation.

U

UNIX

The original **operating system** on which the Internet was developed.

unzip (See **zipped file**)

upload

To copy a file from your computer to another computer on the Internet. If you have your own Web site, chances are you upload your new pages to your ISP's server. Upload is the opposite of **download**.

URL

Stands for Uniform Resource Locator. URL is another term for a Web address. Every page on the Web has its own URL. (See *"Getting Around on the Web."*)

Usenet

A worldwide network of **newsgroups** on over 30,000 different topics. Newsgroups are named with a series of words and periods. For example, `rec.pets.dogs.breeds` is a place where people discuss every breed of dog from pit bulls to Chihuahuas (the `rec` is short for recreation). You can access Usenet newsgroups through Dejanews at `www.dejanews.com`.

user

A person who uses computer software or hardware (as opposed to the person who created the software or hardware).

utility

A small computer program that performs a single, useful function. Many shareware programs are utilities.

V

virtual reality

The simulation of a real or imaginary environment.

virus

Software that attempts to effect your computer without your permission. Viruses do not spontaneously generate; they are written by someone for a specific purpose. Many false warnings, or virus hoaxes, circulate on the Internet. (See *"Staying Smart, Safe, and Secure."*)

W

Web (See **World Wide Web**)

Webcam

A video camera attached to the Internet. Originally, Webcams were aimed at fish tanks and coke machines. Now, the views are more interesting (exotic locations like Hawaii) or more useful (traffic conditions). Take a look at Tommy's List of Live Cams Worldwide at `chili.rt66.com/ozone/countries.htm`.

Webcasting

This term is used in two ways. Just as television shows are broadcast to your television, live and videotaped shows can be Webcast to your browser. Webcasting can also refer to push technology, when news, weather, sports scores, and other timely information is sent to your browser or your desktop.

Web address (See **URL**)

Webmaster

The person or group responsible for a Web site. Usually, you can e-mail the webmaster of any site by addressing your e-mail to the domain name. For example, the webmaster at `www.website.com` can be reached at `webmaster@website.com`.

Web site

A collection of pages at the same **address**, or **URL**, is called a Web site. The first page you come to is called the home page. From there, you can get to the other pages in the site, using hyperlinks.

Web page

A file on the Internet that can be displayed by a browser. Web pages can contain text, graphics, animation, video, and audio. Web pages are generally written in **HTML**. Several related Web pages located at the same address are called a **Web site**.

WebTV

A device that allows you to browse the Web on your TV set with a remote control (and optionally, a wireless keyboard). WebTV has a built-in modem that connects to the Internet through the phone lines and requires you to use a special ISP. WebTV costs between $100 and $250.

wired

Connected to the Internet. *Wired* is also the name of a magazine that covers technology and the culture that surrounds it.

World Wide Web

Invented in 1991 by Tim-Berners Lee, the Web is the fastest growing Internet service. It is made up of many pages, usually containing text and graphics, connected together with **hyper-links**. It is also known as the Web, the WWW, and the W3. For more information, see *Appendix B*.

W3C (World Wide Web Consortium)

An international group that promotes standards for the Web. Originally formed with CERN, where the Web was invented, it is now hosted by the MIT Laboratory for Computer Science and INRIA in Europe. Their Web site is at `www.w3.org`.

WWW (See **World Wide Web**)

WYSIWYG

Stands for "What You See Is What You Get." (Pronounced "whiz ee whig.") In a WYSIWYG editor, you can see what a Web page will look like in a browser while you are working at it. This makes it easier to focus on how the site will look when you are finished.

X

x2

A modem technology that will allow you to transmit data over ordinary phone lines at a maximum speed of 56 Kbps (thousands of bits per second). Another technology, K56flex, is competing to be the new standard. The two technologies are not compatible. If you purchase a 56 Kbps modem, check with your ISP to see which technology they support.

Y

Year 2000 Bug (or "Y2K")

Many computer systems and software programs store the date as two digits instead of four (i.e., "1998" is stored as "98"). These systems will see the year 2000 as "00" and interpret that as 1900 (or even 1980, the earliest year PCs are aware of). Unless these problems are identified and fixed, problems will occur in older, "legacy" systems in many companies as well as the government.

Z

zipped file

Often downloaded software has been compressed into a `.zip` file. A popular Windows program called WinZip can be used to decompress the file. You can download WinZip free at `www.winzip.com`. (See **compression**)

Appendix A

Five Popular Myths About The Internet

The Internet is a hot topic. It is also new, controversial, and easily misunderstood. Television and movies, people you talk to, even major news magazines tend to misrepresent or oversimplify the Internet. As a result, there are many myths and misconceptions that persist.

Take a look at 5 of the most common myths, and the actual truth that lies behind them.

1) You must be "good at computers" to use the Net.

Many people believe that, unless you happen to be a computer whiz, the Internet is just too complicated to use. A few years ago, this was not far from the truth. The Internet has its roots in an operating system called Unix. It required you to remember a lot of cryptic commands. No one "surfed"; you had to know exactly where you were going, and type in the right command to get there.

Now, the World Wide Web has made life on the Internet much easier. User-friendly software is available to help you send e-mail and download files. Connecting to the Internet with your home PC has never been easier. And the Web, with all of its pages linked together with hyperlinks, puts a whole world of information at your fingertips.

Because the Internet is so much easier to use now, people from all walks of life have discovered it. Over the last year, the number of people on the Internet has doubled every 100 days. Most of those people are *not* computer whizzes!

2) The Web is the entire Net.

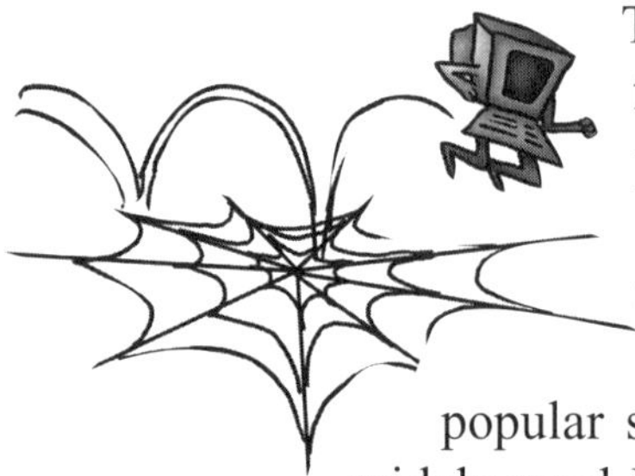

The World Wide Web is by far the fastest growing (and the flashiest) part of the Internet, which is why it gets so much attention. But it is not the only service on the Internet; it is not even the most popular service. E-mail remains the most widely used Internet service. Millions of people log on to the Internet to send and receive e-mail. Many have never seen the Web.

Other popular and useful services include Usenet, ftp (file transfer protocol), and IRC (Internet Relay Chat). See *Appendix B* for an introduction to each of these. The Web is only a part of what the Internet has to offer.

3) If you read it on the Net, it must be true.

Anyone can say anything on the Net. That does not make it true. Information you get from the Internet, whether it comes from e-mail, the Web, or Usenet, must be evaluated carefully. Do you know and trust the source? (The *original* source, not the person who forwarded the message to you.) Does the story make sense? Can you check the story out? Don't believe everything you read, no matter how official it might sound.

Also, the Internet is a great medium for distributing up-to-the-minute information to millions of people. Many individuals (and companies) put informative sites on the Web. But often, that information is left on the Web indefinitely, without any updates. So you can't assume that the information you are reading is current.

4) The Internet is full of pornography.

There are people who use the Internet to distribute pornography, just as they use other methods (like 900 numbers, magazines, TV, and VCRs). But the *amount* of pornography on the Internet is often overestimated and overrepresented.

Cyberporn does exist. But, it is estimated that less than 1% of the messages transmitted across the Internet are related to pornography. So unless you avoid bookstore because of some the magazines and books they carry, there's no reason to avoid the Internet. If you are worried about it, see the section on "protecting your family."

Many people trace this myth back to Time Magazine's 1995 article on Cyberporn. The article quoted statistics from a University study showing a huge percentages of pornography on the Net. The study this article was based on turned out to be from a college freshman, and was discredited. Time Magazine ran a large correction and an apology later, but the impression was already made. [The Cyberporn Report: `www.cybernothing.org/cno/reports/cyberporn.html`**]**

5) The Internet can, and should, be censored and regulated.

The truth is, it is not technically possible to censor the Internet. The Internet is a cooperation of computers around the world. No one person, company, or even government owns the Internet. So no one has the right to regulate it, or the ability to censor it.

The Internet is also a worldwide haven for free speech. This means that you can post anything you would like to say. But it also means that there will be plenty of things said and shown on the Internet that you will not agree with, including pornography and hate messages.

The good news is that the Internet *can* be censored on a local level. There is software and hardware you can buy to protect your children from the wrong content. There are also Internet Service Providers, like America Online and Mayberry USA, who censor the Internet before it reaches your family.

Appendix B

The Internet: Frequently Asked Questions

On the Internet, you come across FAQs all the time. FAQ stands for Frequently Asked Questions. When you are new to a subject, they are a great place to start.

This section contains answers to the questions most people ask (or want to ask!) about the Internet. The answers are written in plain English. If you come across any terms you don't understand, take a look at the glossary of terms in the back of this book.

Let's start with the basics:

1) What is the Internet?

The Internet is made up of millions of computers all over the world, connected together, sharing information.

It's not exactly like an Information Superhighway; but more like the road system of a city (say, New Orleans). There are Interstate highways, major exits, busy intersections, smaller roads, dirt roads, and driveways. There are traffic jams and potholes.

One difference between the Internet and a road system is that, although it might take you close an hour to get from Kenner to New Orleans East (in traffic), it could take you less than a minute to travel through cyberspace to Timbuktu.

Because of this, the Internet is the perfect way to send information like news and weather, instantly, around the world.

2) Is There A Difference Between The Internet And The World Wide Web?

Although the Internet and the Web are often used interchangeably, they are different things. The Web is one of many services available over the Internet. Let's compare the Internet to a road once more. Most people driving on the road during rush hour are commuters. For the most part, they are driving cars to get to and from work. You might see a lot of them on the road. But at the same time, the roads are being used for trucks carrying cargo, and postal trucks carrying mail. Some people are on the road just for fun. You might see a motorcyclist as well. On quieter streets, you will see bicyclists. Joggers. Go-karts. Similarly, the Web is only one type of "Internet traffic" out there.

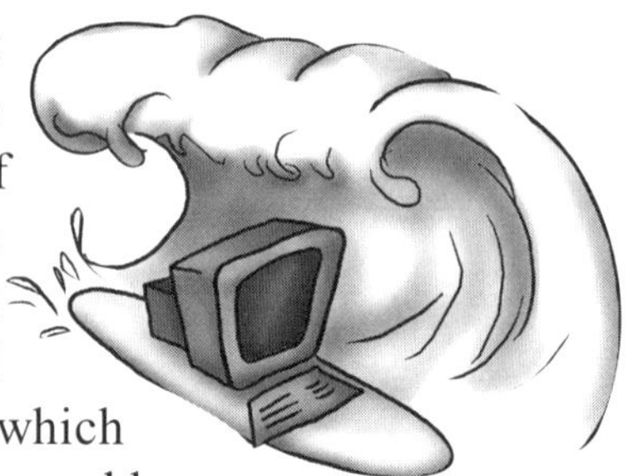

The World Wide Web gets a lot of attention because it is the fastest growing and flashiest of the Internet services. It has been described as the Internet with pictures. First, it combined graphics and text on pages which linked to each other. People were able to navigate between pages and sites easily, with a mouse. Now, Web pages can include audio, video, and animation.

In addition to the World Wide Web, the Internet plays host to several other services. Here is an overview:

E-mail

The web might be the fastest growing Internet service, but e-mail is the most popular. In fact, 84% of Internet users call e-mail "indispensible." Many people access the Internet solely to send and receive e-mail. E-mail is faster than old-fashioned mail, and often more reliable (especially when you are sending a message to another country).

E-mail messages can travel around the world within minutes, or even seconds. E-mail is an inexpensive and convenient way to keep in touch with friends, family, and business associates.

FTP

FTP stands for File Transfer Protocol. FTP allows you to copy a file (like a shareware program, for example) from one computer to another over the Internet. Before the Web, FTP was difficult to use; it required you to type in a whole series of commands. Now, it is built right in to many browsers.

Gopher

Before the Web, there was Gopher. Instead of surfing from page to page, you chose files to view from a menu. Some sites still use Gopher, but you won't see it very often anymore.

Telnet

Telnet gives you direct access to a remote computer. You can then read mail, tranfer files, and run programs. You can use Telnet to access the card catalog at the public library.

Usenet

Usenet is made up of ongoing discussions on just about any topic under the sun. Using newsgroups, you can find the answer to just about any question you have, whether it's about Seinfeld or genetic research.

IRC

IRC stands for Internet Relay Chat. Chat groups are like virtual rooms where people gather to talk about many different topics. You can start your own chat group, or join one of the thousands that already exist.

3) Who Started the Internet?

Birth of the Internet

During the Cold War in the 1960s, the U.S. Government decided to build a network of computers across the country. The network was designed so each computer could send a message to any other computer. A message could find its way across the network, even if part of the network was destroyed. This network was called ARPANET (named after the Advanced Research Projects Agency, part of the Department of Defense)

Universities, with the help defense-related government funding, joined the developing network. Scientists were now able to share research with each other, and they soon outnumbered the government users. Eventually, the responsibility for maintaining the "backbone" of the network transferred from the Department of Defense to the National Science Foundation (it was renamed NSFNet). Throughout the 1980s, universities continued to improve the way the network functioned.

Private companies joined the action in the late 1980s. Business people began to outnumber the scientists. The responsibilities for maintaining the backbone shifted once again in 1995, to a group of private companies. The NSFNet became the Internet as we know it today.

Birth of the Web

Often, people are surprised to learn that the Web has only been around since 1989. It was invented by Tim Berners-Lee, a scientist with a European think tank called CERN (Conseil Europeen pour la Recherche Nucleaire).

Originally, the Web was created to help CERN scientists share research. Pages were "hyperlinked" together, making it easy to look at any document on any computer in the network.

At first, pages on the Web were just plain text. It wasn't until 1993, when a browser called Mosaic was developed, that Web pages could contain pictures. The popularity of the Web began to explode. (The developer of Mosaic, Marc Andresson, went on to cofound Netscape a year later. Netscape created Navigator, one of the two most popular browsers.)

4) How Does the Internet Work?

The main "highways" of the Internet carry the most traffic. Together, they are known as the "backbone." They are owned and maintained by phone companies like MCI and Sprint, and ISPs like America Online. They start from five hub cities (like an airline's hub cities): San Francisco, San Jose, Chicago, New Jersey, and Washington, D.C. They connect to each other, and zigzag across the U.S. and extend around the world. Redundancy means that if any part of the backbone in the U.S. goes down, the network will be re-routed and will still work. In other countries, the backbone is often not as well developed, and no redendancy means breakdowns and slowdowns occur more often.

Regional and local ISPs lease access from the major providers. In turn, when you sign up for access, you connect to the ISP. Looking at it the other way, your small connection to the Internet (like a 28.8 modem, using a phone line) feeds into your ISP's larger, faster connection, (like a T1, which would be 50x as fast) which feeds into the backbone (usually fiber optics, laid by phone companies).

That's how the computers are connected together. But, it is not enough that the computer are networked together (talking to each other). They have to be speaking the same language.

The primary language of the Internet is a "protocol" called TCP/IP. This stands for Transmission Control Protocol and Internet Protocol.

TCP takes information (like an e-mail message) and breaks it down into small pieces, called packets. Each packet is stamped with the name and address of the sender and the receiver.

Then, IP figures out how to get the packets to their destination. The packets are send through a series of "routers," much like a letter sent through the U.S. mail passes through several post offices before it gets to your house. Each router looks at the address on the packet, and sends the packet along to its next stop along the way. This means, that if you have a long e-mail message taht got broken into several packets, they might have all taken a different route to get to you. When they arrive at their destination, TCP checks all the packets, and assembles them together for you.

Although TCP/IP is the main Internet protocol, there are others. For example, the Internet uses a protocol called HTTP to transmit Web pages. (See *"How Does the Web Work?"*)

5) How Does the Web Work?

The Web is a collection of pages, linked together. A group of pages in one location is called a Web site. A page on the Web can link to any other page in any other location, using a "hyperlink."

Web pages can be made up of text, pictures, audio, video, or other information. Pages are sent across the Internet using a protocol called HTTP (Hypertext Transfer Protocol). You can think of HTTP as a set of rules that govern how computers exchange text, pictures, audio, and video.

Web pages are written in HTML (Hypertext Markup Language). When you click on a hyperlink, your brower sends a request across the Internet, asking for a particular Web page. The page is then sent back to your computer, similar to the way e-mail messages are sent (see *"How Does the Internet Work?"*) Your browser reads the HTML, and figures out how to display the text, graphics (pictures) and other information on your screen.

6) Who Controls the Internet?

Although the Internet was initially created with funding from the Department of Defense, the National Science Foundation, and several universities, there is no organization which "owns" the Internet. The Internet works because many organizations around the world provide computers which cooperate and share information with each other.

Many companies, institutions, and governments donate time, people, and money to keep the Internet going. Several independent groups have been formed to guide the development of the Internet and set technology standards for companies to follow.

Remember, information on the Internet is forwarded from one computer to another until it reaches its destination. Every computer connected to the Internet becomes part of the chain. So, every company linked to the Internet helps foot the bill. And when you sign up for Internet access with an Internet Service Provider (an ISP), you are effectively helping to pay for the Internet as well.

No one person, agency, company, or government owns the Internet. So it is difficult, if not impossible, for any government to regulate it, even the government that started it (the U.S. government). It is no wonder the Internet is changing the way the world communicates.

IMPRESS YOUR FRIENDS!

Here are a few of the groups involved in guiding the development of the Internet:

The World Wide Web Consortium (W3C) sets standards for HTML, the language Web pages are written in.

The Internet Engineering Task Force (IETF) focuses on the evolution of the Internet with a specific eye toward keeping the Internet running smoothly as a whole.

The Internet Engineering Steering Group (IESG) is concerned with keeping the Internet running smoothly.

The Internet Network Information Center (InterNIC) assigns domain names to Web sites.

7) Why is the Web So Slow?

Actually, it is amazingly fast. An e-mail you send now can arrive in Timbuktu in seconds.

So why are there so many times when you click on a link to get the latest sports scores, and you wait ... and wait ... and wait?

The answer has to do with something called bandwidth. Bandwidth refers to the amount of information that can be carried on the Internet. Remember the analogy of the road system? When the "roads" of the Internet were first constructed, there were very few "cars" out there. Basically, the government, universities, and a few cutting-edge companies were the only traffic. Now, with so many people online, there are traffic jams and slowdowns, especially at peak times. And the problem is just getting worse: studies show that the number of people online doubles every 100 days!

But that's not the whole story. Web pages have become more complex, with more graphics, animation, video, audio, and programs like Java. Companies use the latest technology to spice up their Web pages, and so they use much more bandwidth. So, in addition to more people on the Web, there is more complex information being transmitted. To understand how this effects bandwidth, it might be helpful to think of the Internet as a series of pipes. The pipes are very thick. All of the information that is sent over the Internet - like e-mail and Web pages - is like water. There used to be only a trickle of water, in a very wide pipe. Now, there is a flood of water, and the pipe is not any wider than it once was. Every time you send an email or visit (request) a Web page, you add to the load the Internet has to handle.

Add to that the things that can go wrong with equipment, from lightening striking the telephone pole outside your house to part of the backbone going down, and you can see why the Internet can be somewhat unpredictable.

Every year, new techology is introduced to increase the bandwidth of the Internet. And every year, newer and more high-tech information is sent across the Internet, using up the bandwidth. It seems that, no matter how much bandwidth we have, it is never quite enough.

If you're not happy about this, imagine how the government agencies and universities who created the Internet feel. What used to be a quick way for them to share information has become a traffic jam full of everyone from your 8-year old neighbor to your grandmother. So the government is developing Internet II, a super-fast backbone network. It will not replace the existing Internet, but it will provide alternate routes for universities and government agencies, so they can avoid the increasing commercial traffic. (Like a carpool lane on the highway.)

8) How Big Is The Internet?

Huge. At the end of 1997, there were an estimated 100 million people on the Internet. About 327 million people are expected to be online by the year 2000 (although some etimates say the number will be closer to 700 million). About 40 percent of those, or 132 million, will be here in the U.S. (Compare that to only 1 million people who were online at the end of 1994!)

Estimates put the number of Web sites at well over 150 million. (In June 1993, there were only a handful of Web sites – less than 200.)

For the latest statistics, go to `www.mediamatrix.com`.

9) If There's So Much Out There, Why Can't I Find What I Need?

One of the most amazing things about the Internet is the tremendous amount of information that it holds. Whether you are wondering how the government spends tax dollars, you need to know the weather forecast for the city of Goteborg, Sweden, or you are wondering if Madonna's mole is real, there is plenty of useful (and not-so-useful) information right at your fingertips. And the Web continues to grow, as hundreds of thousands of Web pages are added every day.

The problem is, there is so much information, and so many new pages added every day, that finding what you need is like looking for a needle in the biggest haystack in the world. There is no central place to register what web sites are about. And there is no central information desk to ask for directions. There is no card catalog and no helpful librarians.

You can use a search engine. Search engines attempt to catalog every word on every web page. When you type in a word, a search engine will return every page that contains that word in any context.

Unfortunately, sometimes that just makes it harder to find what you need. Typing in a common word like "vacation" might give you millions of pages to sift through. Surfing through all those sites to find just the information you need would be frustrating and time consuming.

For example, imagine you are looking for advice on building a deck in your backyard. Try typing in "building decks." You'll find sites about card games, companies who refinish boat decks, and — if you're lucky — that advice you are looking for, buried under everything. You might have to do a lot of searching before you find the page you need.

To help out, some search engines try to prioritize the results. They might count how many times the word is mentioned in a page. Or they might use special sections of the page to classify the page. This way, they can give you a page that is more relevent. But Web authors know this, they can play tricks with the system, pushing their site higher in the results even through their page might not be what you were looking for.

To add to the problem, search engines contain references to pages that are out of date, have changed, or no longer even exist. Since "searching" doesn't necessarily mean "finding," it can be a very frustrating experience.

See *"Finding What You Need"* for some tips that make searching the Internet much easier.

10) What's the Difference Between America Online and the Internet?

Actually, the lines are blurring. Before the Web, customers signed on to America Online, Prodigy, CompuServe, and other networks. These private networks offered consumer information, email, communities of people sharing common interests, software, etc. They charged by the minute or the hour. They all looked different, worked differently, and had their own software to access them. They connected to vast networks that were only open to their customers. They added unique content and services in order to compete with each other.

But then the Web came along, and grew in popularity. The Web was a much bigger network than any online service could provide. The interface was the same for everyone — a browser. The network wasn't owned by any one company. The online services found they were in competition with the ISPs who offered Web access.

Slowly, the large commercial online services began to change. They started to charge a flat rate instead of an hourly rate. They offered access to the Web as well as to their own content. Slowly, they changed over to become ISPs, giving people access to the content growing on the Web, rather than offering their own content.

Only America Online now maintains its own network. The others are ISPs who charge you for Web access, and offer parts of their Web sites only to members. Now, instead of paying for access to a private network, you are paying for Web access, plus extra content offered by the ISP. So you must evaluate them like any other ISP (see *"How Do I Get Online"* for tips on choosing an ISP).

Appendix C - LIST OF ISPs

Local & regional

ISP Name	*Telephone*	*Web Site*	*Monthly Fee*
Acadian Internet	(504) 888-1236	www.acadiacom.net	$18.75
AccessCom	(504) 887-0022	www.accesscom.net	
AssurTech/NterNet Inc.	(800) 960-4106	www.nternet.com	
Bellsouth.net	(800) 4DOTNET	www.bellsouth.net/external	$19.95
Beyond 2000	(504) 887-2000	www.b2k.net	$19.95
Cajun Net	(504) 868-7856	www.cajun.net	
FirstNet of Acadiana	(318) 289-0125	www.1stnet.com	$25.00
Greater New Orleans FreeNet	(504) 529-5576	www.gnofn.org	none
Gulf Coast Internet Co.	(800) 444-4638	www.gulf.net	$20.00
I-10 Netway	(504) 885-0033	www.i-10.net	$24.95
I-55 Internet	(504) 345-1170	www.i-55.com	$24.95
Lanyap Internet Services	(504) 522-0708	www.lanyap.com	$25.00
LinkNet Internet Services	(318) 449-4622	www.linknet.net	$19.95
Neosoft	(888) 636-7638	www.neosoft.com	
Southern Star	(504) 888-3348	www.sstar.com	$25.00
Verio Gulf South	(504) 527-6200	gulfsouth.verio.net	

National ISPs

ISP Name	*Telephone*	*Web Site*	*Monthly Fee*
AT&T Worldnet Service	800/967-5363	www.worldnetall.com	$19.95
Blue Sky Internet	503-669-1497	www.blueskyweb.com	$19.95
EarthLink Network	800/395-8425	www.earthlink.net	$19.95
IBM Global Network	800/775-5808	www.ibm.net	
LDS iAmerica	800-789-6062	www.iamerica.net	$19.95
MCI	800-348-8011	www.mci2000.com	$19.95
MindSpring Enterprises	800/719-4332	www.mindspring.com	$19.95
Prodigy Internet	800-213-0992	www.prodigy.com	$19.95
Sprint Internet Passport	800-359-3900	www.sprint.com/sip	$19.95
UUNET Technologies	800-4UUNET4	www.uu.net	$30.00

Commercial Online Services

ISP Name	*Telephone*	*Web Site*	*Monthly Fee*
America Online	888-265-8001	www.aol.com	$21.95
Compuserve	800-524-3388	www.compuserve.com	$24.95
MSN Premier	800-386-5550	www.msn.com	$19.95

Did you enjoy this book? Let us know at our web site:

`www.learntheweb.com`

While you are there, pick up some extra copies for Mom and Dad, your grandparents, and your aunts and uncles. They make great gifts!